HANDBOOK FOR PEER MINISTRY

Joseph Moore
&
James P. Emswiler

PAULIST PRESS   *New York/Ramsey*

Acknowledgements

Excerpt from *Awareness: Exploring, Experimenting, Experiencing,* by John O. Stevens, © 1971. Real People Press. Used by permission.

Excerpt from *Peer Program for Youth* by Ardyth Hebeisen. Used by permission of Search Institute, Minneapolis, Minnesota.

Excerpt from *Awareness Experience for School Use* by Bette Hamlin. Used by permission of Cebco Standard Publishing.

Excerpt from Designs in Affective Education by Elizabeth W. Flynn and John F. LaFaso. © 1974 by Elizabeth W. Flynn and John F. LaFaso. Reprinted by permission of Paulist Press.

Excerpt from *Religion in America: 1979–80.* Used with permission of the Princeton Religion Research Center.

Excerpt from *The Velveteen Rabbit* by Margery Williams, New York: Doubleday & Co., Inc., 1958.

Photo credits:
Bob Combs, p. xii; Rising Hope, p. 20; Alan Cliburn, p. 34; Paul Buddle, p. 80. *Cover photo credits:* Alan Cliburn, Paul Conklin, and Camerique.

Library of Congress
Catalog Card Number: 81-84351

ISBN: 0-8091-2427-0

Published by Paulist Press
545 Island Road, Ramsey, N.J. 07446

Printed and bound in the
United States of America

CONTENTS

APPENDIX

THANK YOU

We wish to express thanks to Kevin Cayer who suggested the peer ministry approach to us when he was fifteen years old; and thanks to Betty Dahill, Betty Lecza, James Branigan, C.S.C., Peggy Fromme, S.U.S.C. and the Peer Ministry teams, St. George Parish Community, Guilford, Connecticut; special thanks to Merton Strommen for his research and inspiration.

FOREWORD

This book shows how a Christian educator can move beyond the traditional stance of nurturing and sheltering youth to equipping and employing them in a strategic ministry.

It addresses the growing need for training programs that equip youth, parents, and adult leaders for a sensitive and responsible ministry to hurting people. It describes in a beautiful way what ought to become a permanent feature and dimension of a congregational youth ministry.

Scholars in the helping professions have found that limited periods of training are sufficient to equip lay persons for significant though limited counseling (or friendship) ministries. In many public schools children in upper grades are being equipped through peer counselor training to do cross-age tutoring with disadvantaged or younger children.

The authors of this book, Joseph Moore and James Emswiler, have skillfully assembled key ideas and practical information on how to establish a peer ministry in congregation or school. An insightful, realistic approach to integrating what could become a powerful addition to an ongoing youth ministry, it provides both the rationale and specific helps needed to begin such a program.

The urgency for this program is seen in the quiet crisis occurring among most of the mainline denominations. Since the 1960's there has been a steady decline in Church membership and Church school enrollment, the first in a century or two characterized by Church growth. Much of this decline can be accounted for by a disproportionately large number of dropouts among members under the age of thirty. Though dropouts from Church have always been common among teenagers and young adults, they tripled during the 1960's and doubled during the 1970's. It is unlikely that many of these will wander back into the Church unless they are reached by persons who take their peer ministry seriously.

What is presented in this book will be useful for all ages in reaching people of their own age and level. We have found that there is a special advantage for people reaching out to people who care closest to them in status, age, and training. Few are more effective in reaching early adolescents than those who are high school age; few are more effective in reaching youth of high school age than young adults. Training in a peer ministry is a natural way of extending and multiplying the ministry of a local congregation or school.

Merton P. Strommen, Ph.D.
May 15, 1981

DEDICATION

For Doug Farrina

and

for Frank Chauvin,
peer minister and friend

1 | WHY PEER MINISTRY?

"He's losing his faith!" his mother cried out.

"I can't understand it," his parish priest said. "We have a folk Mass every Sunday, a CYO basketball team, and courses on sacraments and Church history, but the kids just won't come out."

"Look at that gang," his neighbors scowled. "They talk alike, they dress alike, they think alike. They're like a herd of cows."

"You know," he said. "I don't think I believe that religious stuff anymore."

In human terms, these are the reasons behind peer ministry. The psychological and emotional passages of adolescence are so turbulent, complex and confusing that the faith passage is caught in the backlash. Our past approaches in religious education and youth ministry often appeared to be set apart from the young person's holistic development. And while religion textbooks on the elementary level are now being written in light of developmental research, adolescent programs continue to be feared as the proverbial potatoes that few wish to handle for fear of being burned.

This book is a practical response to research on the adolescent developmental process. It takes the literature of emotional, psychological, moral, and faith theories and applies it to a program designed for the youth of an apparent "turned-off" generation. It is not the only program available for adolescent faith development, but it is one that is solidly based and spiritually alive. Most important, it is a program that has been tested and proven successful.

Peer ministry is basically common sense. People who are around the same age in life and who have passed recently through an experience are often the best ones to help others through the same experience. This is true during the teenage years as it is in other stages of life. Peers have been ministering to peers since the beginning of time. Those of us old enough to remember can probably recall some young adult or older teenager who helped us through our own adolescence. Nonetheless, it is supportive in this complex age when there are so many opinions about everything to find that researchers in the area of human development agree with the peer ministry approach.

THE SEARCH FOR IDENTITY

Every young person experiences a need to break away from the dependence of earlier years in order to stand on his/her own two feet. This breaking away is often characterized by a rebellion that can range from the barely noticeable to the violent revolution. And, as with any rebellion, the participant will turn, not to the authority, but to the peer group in order to achieve independence. The colonists did not attend real estate classes by King George to gain their freedom from England. In the same way, young people look to their peers, not their parents and parish priests, when they are searching for an identity to call their own.

> This does not signify distrust or lack of love. It is simply easier for them to come to terms with themselves with those to whom they are less emotionally attached. Some youngsters, of course, turn to outsiders because their parents are unempathic, disrespectful, and refuse to give up their power. But even those with empathic, democratic parents often prefer working through some of their feelings with people outside the family.[1]

And like the American tourist returning to England today, the rebellious young person does come back again.

The identity crisis is a normal and necessary part of an individual's development. It is a passage that each of us must travel on our road to complete personhood. We are grateful to psychologist Erik Erikson for his insights on the identity crisis. Like recent findings on heart disease and high blood pressure, these insights will not make the crisis disappear, but will assist its treatment and control. In *Identity and the Life Cycle,* Erikson outlines a series of eight passages, or crises, that individuals go through as they mature. The fifth crisis, which normally occurs during the period of adolescence, is termed identity versus identity diffusion. Young people must experience a continuity between their past life and their future role. In every aspect of their personalities, they are shedding childhood notions and achieving adult capabilities.

> Reevaluation means refocusing on autonomy, initiative, attachment, and personal and social mastery. But this

3

second time around, the teen-ager needs answers as a budding adult rather than as a child. The major task of adolescence is the reevaluation of self.

Reworking his identity is of far greater importance to the adolescent than learning the intricacies of calculus or the sonnets of Shakespeare. We all know the brilliant adult—the precocious quiz kid parading his facts—whose life bogs down because he lacks a solid sense of identity. He finds little meaning in life and cannot relate successfully to others. A factual sponge, he knows all about the "world out there" while his inner world remains a puzzle.[2]

Like the rest of us, young adults look to others for support and assistance during a crisis. And, as mentioned above, it is the peer group to whom they look first and foremost. Thus, the need for trained individuals to help their peers weather the crisis. In *Identity, Youth, and Crisis,* Erikson states that "the relative waning of the parents and the emergence of the young adult specialist as the permanent and permanently changing authority is bringing about a shift by which older youth guided by such young authority will have to take increasing responsibility for the orientation of the specialists and of older youth. This, however, we can only do by recognizing and cultivating an age-specific ethical capacity in older youth, which is the true criterion of identity."[3]

For the young person in search of an identity, even falling in love is a way of bouncing off another the problems, the questions, and the confusion of this phase. "To a considerable extent, adolescent love is an attempt to arrive at a definition of one's identity by projecting one's diffused self-image on another and by seeing it thus reflected and gradually clarified. This is why so much of young love is conversation."[4]

In short, the adolescent is suffering from the pangs of

growth and searching for an identity. The young man at the beginning of this chapter is struggling to find a continuity between his past and future. He is crying out for help in his struggle, but he cannot look to his parents, his pastor, or his neighbors anymore. Who will help him?

THE NEED FOR COMMUNITY

> The young adolescent craves group acceptance even more than he did during the middle years. Fourteen-year-old Sam knows the answer to the question asked in class, but he says he doesn't. Why? He wants to be one of the boys and being too smart is frowned on by his crowd. With the insecurity that comes from reshuffling his identity, the young teen-ager needs large transfusions of confirmation from friends.[5]

The young person in search of identity, both secular and religious, needs community. But he won't normally discover this particular community in church and he won't find it amid the theological principles of organized religion. Identity will be worked out in the peer group hanging around the corner drugstore. Here is the ecclesia of adolescence. Conversation is the ritual, ultimate acceptance the greatest sacrament.

"Parents and youth leaders who view the peer group objectively also see its values and importance. There is no better place for the youth to learn the skills of interpersonal relationships between equals. Social adjustments are more frequently made in social situations than in classroom or academic learning experience. Learning to relate by relating in an accepting surrounding is the better way. A basic part of this learning is the 'untying of apron strings'—the moving from a parent-centered world to an other-centered way of life."[6]

Moving to other-centeredness is the goal of Christianity,

5

and it can be achieved only within community. In the New Testament (see John 13:3–17) we see Jesus, the master teacher, motivating his peers to minister to others. He knew that the Father had given him complete power; he knew that he had come from God and was going to God. So he rose from the table, took off his outer garment, and tied a towel around his waist. Then he poured some water into a washbasin and began to wash the disciples' feet and dry them with the towel around his waist. He came to Simon Peter, who said to him, "Are you going to wash my feet, Lord?" Jesus answered him, "You do not understand now what I am doing, but you will understand later." Peter declared, "Never at any time will you wash my feet!"

"If I do not wash your feet," Jesus answered, "you will no longer be my disciple."

Simon Peter answered, "Lord, do not wash only my feet, then! Wash my hands and head, too!"

Jesus said, "Anyone who has taken a bath is completely clean and does not have to wash himself, except for his feet. All of you are clean—all except one." (Jesus already knew who was going to betray him; that is why he said, "All of you, except one, are clean.") After Jesus had washed their feet, he put his outer garment back on and returned to his place at the table. "Do you understand what I have just done to you?" he asked.

"You call me Teacher and Lord, and it is right that you do so, because that is what I am. I, your Lord and Teacher, have just washed your feet. You, then, should wash one another's feet. I have set an example for you, so that you will do just what I have done for you. I am telling you the truth; no slave is greater than his master, and no messenger is greater than the one who sent him. Now that you know this truth, how happy you will be if you put it into practice."

Helping others get through their problems and giving

each other support and encouragement is what Jesus meant by washing another's feet and what we mean by peer ministry.

The desire for community can be an overwhelming need for young people in transition. Merton Strommen, in his Youth Research Survey, asked participants to choose opportunities that a Church could provide for them. The highest preference among low self-esteem youth was a tie between finding meaning in life and *learning how to make friends and be a friend*.

> Three out of four want to be "more of the real me" in a group. They want help in finding friends and learning to be friends to members of both sexes. Friends are to them what bread is to the hungry and clothes to the naked.
>
> What is needed is a ministry of friendship—activities that bring people together to interact.
>
> Three out of four want to be part of a caring, accepting group. Two out of three want a group that, in addition to offering acceptance, also confronts one another with an honest, frank sharing of personal feelings. They want small-group experiences that get at the feeling level and help them to come out from under their public posture.[7]

The need to belong to a caring, accepting group is real. But what happens when the group does not accept a certain young person? The crowd can work either as an enabler or as a destroyer. While the former enables the young person to achieve an identity, the latter destroys all remaining feelings of worth and self-esteem. As anyone who has observed the patterns of adolescent growth knows, kids can be brutally cruel. If a particular individual doesn't have the necessary tribal traits—good looks, outgoing personality, lots of dates, exceptional marks, athletic ability, or whatever—he/she can be locked out of the group in merciless fashion.

> Most adolescents go through periods of feeling quite worthless, especially following some disappointing experience in their friendships or having failed to measure up to others in school grades or sports activities. Such feelings usually pass over like clouds. If they persist and dominate, they become destructive because excessive self-criticism tears down self-esteem and interferes with relationships.

> Such youth especially need to experience the acceptance and love of others. An atmosphere of mutual acceptance can free them to deal with their negative perceptions and feelings of personal guilt.[8]

This is where the Church comes in. As a caring, accepting group which is open to all at any time, the Church can offer a setting for young people in transition. This setting can best be provided, not by Church leaders or adults, but by the young people themselves. Church leaders and adults can *train* young people, but should leave the ministering to the peer group.

In the past, we ignored this process. Young adults were dragged to church to be formed, liturgically or educationally, by those in authority. Even the sacrament of confirmation became some kind of initiation rite which bestowed upon the recipient a new, mature identity of Christian faith. But we forgot the middleman, and in the area of identity formation, the middleman—the peer—is a vital necessity. God understood the process. He sent Jesus.

This is peer ministry—Church leaders training youths to minister to other youths. It is a concept underscored by the documents of bishops around the world. Vatican II proclaimed that "[young people] themselves ought to become the prime and direct apostles of youth, exercising the apostolate among themselves and through themselves and reckoning with the social environment in which they live."[9] The National Conference of Catholic Bishops stated that "all those involved in Catholic youth work should recognize the value of what is called peer group ministry. . . . Young people should be welcomed as co-workers in this genuinely prophetic form of education, and programs which develop their leadership talents should have a central place in the youth ministry."[10]

Peer ministry is an answer to the adolescent's cry for help. It is one way that the Church can respond to the needs of her younger members. It is a way of reaching the youth we thought were gone. And it works.

THE GOAL OF PEER MINISTRY

We have seen in the past few pages that young people undergo a crisis in their lives that can best be resolved by members of their own culture. We have proposed a method called peer ministry to facilitate this resolution. How does peer ministry work?

The theory is simple. If we take a person who has just weathered a critical period and place him/her with someone experiencing the same crisis, the results can be very effective. This method is used in such programs as Weight Watchers, Alcoholics Anonymous, and support groups for the divorced and separated. Obviously a priest can counsel me on my marital problems, but the person who has just been through it can do it better. And I'd rather discuss it with my friend over a drink than with a counselor in a cold clinic.

The same is true with young people. The priest, the religion teacher, or the parent can help them through the identity crisis, but their peers can do it better. All they need is a little training and they can share the joys and sorrows of adolescence with those around them. They can help their peers in the search for meaning in life as well as their reshaping of religious concepts. For Henri Nouwen, this is ministry.

> Ministry means the ongoing attempt to put one's own search for God, with all the moments of pain and joy, despair and hope, at the disposal of those who want to join this search but do not know how. . . . We lay down our life to give new life. . . . We realize that young people call for Christians who are willing to develop their sensitivity to God's presence in their own lives, as well as the lives of others, and to offer their experience as a way of recognition and liberation to their fellow people.[11]

Although any of us can share those moments of pain and joy, despair and hope, we share them more closely with those experiencing the same traumatic moments. These moments for adolescents are filled with concern and fear over their worth and self-esteem. Alleviating the concern and dispelling the fear is the goal of peer ministry.

It is becoming almost trite to say that we must like ourselves before we can love others, but until we can build up our self-esteem, we will have a difficult time relating to others or to God. If adult leaders build a sense of worth in a group of young people, the latter will be able to relate comfortably with their peers and emerge as viable leaders themselves.

> The stronger the youngster's sense of personal worth, the more secure he feels in his group, the easier it is for him to base his decisions on *personal conviction* rather than on the need for group approval. The lower his self-respect, the less he belongs, the stronger the temptation to go along with group pressures to win a place for himself.[12]

Young people who can't find strong role models in peers and significant adults will drift from one stimulus to another, trying to find meaning in their lives. The synthetic stimuli of drugs, sex, and music cannot provide the lasting force given by caring, accepting others. Perhaps Dorothy Corkille Briggs explains it best:

> Up against these barriers, it is small wonder that many young people, blindly groping for the way to meet their needs, have chosen to withdraw through drugs, drop out of a society that doesn't help them in their struggle, or turned to uncommitted sexual release. These behaviors are but symptoms. *We need to focus on the real villain: the feelings, "I am unlovable; I don't matter or belong; I am not capable of coping."*

> If ever there were a time when young people needed a central core of stability, now is that time. The teen-ager who has a faith in himself (born of past successes with life and love) will be less likely to buckle under from outside pressures. The surer he is that he is lovable and worthy, the less security he will need from his environment.

> So many of our young people are serious and tense. We see this in their dancing; it seems more a release from frantic tension than an expression of the joy of movement. Is it significant that teen-agers today dance apart from their partners? Is it perhaps symbolic of the alienation from others that so characterizes our modern society?

> And what is their password? *Love.* In one word they are calling for the curative medicine they need—not only to like themselves, but to feel less tense, less alienated. They need love to scale the hurdles our society has erected. Rapidly becoming a significant majority in our country,

young people are asking for a larger degree of control over their own destinies. They are reaching out for respect and recognition. They are telling us they want to belong by having a voice and to contribute meaningfully to the institutions that affect them. *They are asking for personal involvement to counteract the forces that tell them they have no identity.* [13]

Faith in themselves, so they can share it with others and open it to a new-found understanding of God—this is the result of peer ministry. And it can be initiated by that "central core of stability," the Church.

How do we know it will work? When Merton Strommen surveyed his group of youngsters involved in the Youth Reaching Youth program he discovered two major results:

1. Self-esteem increased dramatically, and self-criticism and personal anxiety decreased.
2. The youth increased measurably in their openness to people and ideas; they learned to share themselves with parents and to be more self-disclosing with their clergymen. [14]

Young people helping other young people along the road to security and strong identity so they can love others and their God—if that isn't religious education and youth ministry at its finest, we don't know what is.

EMPIRICAL VALIDITY

New religion programs are often rooted well in theological and pedagogical theory, but empirical findings to reinforce them are either non-existent or ignored. The concept of peer ministry appears to be justified by statistical data recently reported by two groups of researchers.

In 1976, a paper entitled "Religion and American Youth: With Emphasis on Catholic Adolescents and Young Adults" was published by the United States Catholic Conference. The study, completed by the Boys Town Center for the Study of Youth Development at the Catholic University of America, "profiles the current religious attitudes of Catholic youth and young adults in the United States."

The initial finding of the study was that 90% of American youth believe in a personal God or a higher power of some kind. Despite this incredibly high rate of belief among adolescents, most young people are not overly excited about the offerings of organized religion. They may turn off church attendance (weekly observance dropped from 69% in 1951 to 44% in 1975 in the Boys Town survey; Catholic youth decreased from 81% to 55%), but that, in itself, is no indication of a loss of faith.

> There is no inherent reason why increasing age should lead to loss of faith. Certainly exposure to competing world-views and value systems increases, but religious education can be adapted to mental age and to the market place of ideas. In fact, Goldman believes that how adolescents are taught is as important as what they are taught and that most adolescents "have stopped thinking about religion long before they consciously reject it. The cause of this is a tangle of boredom, the association of religion with fairy tales, 'science has proved religion isn't true,' its apparent remoteness from life . . . and a confusion with much of the language and thought used in the Bible" [*Readiness for Religion* (New York: Seabury Press, 1970), p. 165]. Some of these problems may be remedied by sound teaching programs adapted to the mental age of the developing adolescent, who often feels the need to question beliefs previously accepted, to discuss and to explore. If such personal confrontation with reli-

gious truth is encouraged, the decline in religiousness as the adolescent grows older may be arrested to some extent (p. 11).

In other words, we've got a group of heavy believers who want an update on this "God" concept, but we don't know how to handle it. If numbers are any indication, and we believe they are, our educational approaches to young people fail miserably once they reach their high school years. To substantiate that statement, the Boys Town study states that "90 percent of the 13 to 18 year olds have studied religion at some time or other in their lives, but only 44 percent are now doing so" (p. 11).

Since we have tried everything from lectures to rap groups and Bible study sessions to retreats, perhaps we should acknowledge that the people, not the programs, are missing the mark. The study underscores the point we have been trying to make all along, and it documents it with still other findings.

Loveless and Lodato (1963) discovered a convergence of values in individuals from different religions during adolescence, reflecting a decline in the influence of parents and a growing influence of the peer group. Whitam (1968) performed a follow-up study on teenagers who had "decided for Christ" and documented the importance of friends in the retention of a religious commitment. The relevance of the peer group in explaining values and behavior has been amply demonstrated (see, for example, Elder, 1975; Kandel and Less, 1972) (p. 18).

Peers will reach out to each other in some way—that much is certain. Whether their offer is drugs, sex, or Jesus could depend upon their identity formation and training. Peer ministers will have been formed in the values of Jesus and will

14

attempt to pass them on to their friends. Peer ministry may have arrived just in time, as the conclusion of the study on 13 to 18 year-olds suggests:

> The problems of religion usually associated with college youth have now become the problems of high school youth. Concern for basic values of autonomy and independence has reached within their ranks and affected their religious orientation. They appear less traditional than in the past and a confrontation with faith appears to occur much earlier. Religion seems more peripheral to their lives but the great majority are not alienated from organized religion. They are children of the times who will insist on religious dialogue and not simply religious indoctrination. They are also confused by the very freedom they demand. Support systems of the family and/or peer groups will be important factors in how they react to this freedom. Organized religion, in union with these support systems, can be a major force but today's adolescent will assess it more critically than in the past (p. 21).

The other study, performed by the Princeton Religion Research Center, is entitled "Religion in America 1979–80." In the introduction, George Gallup claims the same initial findings as the Boys Town study, namely that young people "are highly religious although at the same time somewhat turned off by *organized* religion" (p. 3). The researcher then goes on to say that there is great cause for optimism since most adolescents are interested in pulling away from their self-centeredness and entering the "helping" professions in the future.

Gallup reinforces our theory that young people should be trained as ministers:

> Numerous surveys have indicated among young people both a powerful surge of spirituality and a strong interest

15

in service to others. It therefore behooves the churches to join these two strong impulses. Survey evidence indicates that young people would be responsive to various and new kinds of lay ministries—we have para-lawyers and para-medics; perhaps it would be possible to develop para-clerics. Young people might even be given a certain amount of formal training to prepare them for more intense involvement in the functions of the church. Youth should be given the opportunity to serve, but many would maintain that for this service to be truly effective and meaningful, it must be inspired and energized by a strong religious faith. Whatever kinds of ministries are developed, the churches must move quickly to appeal to a generation of youth who are searching for new forms of religion to escape the stultifying effects of a materialistic society (pp. 4–5).

Despite the need, Gallup reiterates the failure of churches to reach out to youth. The study discovered that two-thirds of the young people surveyed blamed the churches for not reaching out and not having enough youth programs.

If an exclamation point can be added to the conclusion of this chapter, let it be marked by this statistical survey which sums up the crying need for peer ministry as soon as possible. It truly says it all.

1. Each church should perhaps consider developing a special ministry to teen-agers. At present, some churches virtually ignore this age group, concentrating on the pre-teens and adults, assuming that the churches cannot compete with all the other interests of teen-agers. And when staff are assigned to this age group, they are often temporary or part-time personnel. This lack of effort to reach teen-agers may sometimes be based on the belief that all churches have to do is to wait until these young

16

people grow older, get married and raise children and then they'll be back in church. But the fact is that there is no guarantee that a teen-ager who today is disenchanted with the church will not stay disenchanted, unless he is given compelling reasons to express his religious feelings with the context of organized religion.

In addition, churches would not wait for teen-agers to appear at the church door but should reach out to these young people, wherever they are.

2. Survey results indicate that teen-agers should be given greater spiritual nourishment. Youth appear to want to explore the depths of their faith and to learn more about prayer and meditation methods. They seek spiritual discipline and want a deeper level of involvement than activities or recreation.

3. Churches should consider developing specific activities for teen-agers to provide an outlet for their apparent religious zeal.

It would appear to be important for organized religion to develop new programs to channel the spirituality of young people into meaningful service on behalf of their fellow men. Not only might youth be encouraged to become involved in the church in a formal way, in the clergy, but also in terms of other forms of service. Study should be given various new forms of ministry, both formal and informal. Indeed, we have para-lawyers and para-medics—perhaps it would be possible to develop para-clerics. Young people might be given a certain amount of formal training and thus become more involved in the functions of the church than they are at present.

Whatever the kinds of religious vocations and ministries developed, it would appear that our churches must move quickly and decisively to appeal to a generation of youth who are searching for new forms and new ways of escaping from the dulling effects of what many regard as a highly materialistic society.

From the point of view of church leaders, the time to act is now. At this very moment, across the land, there are thousands of young people who, finding their own churches sterile and spiritually unrewarding, are joining the ranks of the unchurched or are opting for the nearest fad religion or self-proclaimed messiah.

It is also important for churches to make strenuous efforts to reach the teen-age population since many young people (in fact, half of high school graduates) will go on to college and therefore be subject to the secularizing effects of college.

To be sure, the college experience represents a period of healthy introspection. Yet the fact remains that, in the case of many students, there is a pronounced—and, in some cases, permanent—decline in religious belief and practice between freshman and senior years. A steady fall-off is recorded in the proportion of students who believe in God and in life after death. The percentage who say their religious beliefs are "very important" declines. The proportion who say they have no religious preferences doubles by senior year, while the rate of church attendance is cut nearly in half (p. 66).

NOTES

1. Dorothy Corkille Briggs, *Your Child's Self-Esteem* (Garden City: Doubleday, 1970), p. 159.

2. *Ibid.,* pp. 154–155.

3. Erik Erikson, *Identity, Youth, and Crisis* (New York: W. W. Norton Co., 1968), Prologue.

4. Gloria Durka, "Identity—The Major Task of Adolescence," G. Temp Sparkman, ed., *Knowing and Helping Youth* (Nashville: Broadman Press, 1977), pp. 22–23.

5. Briggs, *op. cit.,* p. 155.

6. Robert E. Poerschke, "Adolescents in the Family and Subculture," G. Temp Sparkman, ed., *Knowing and Helping Youth* (Nashville: Broadman Press, 1977), p. 38.

7. Merton Strommen, *The Five Cries of Youth* (San Francisco: Harper and Row, 1974), p. 27.

8. *Ibid.,* p. 17.

9. *Decree on the Apostolate of the Laity,* n. 12.

10. *To Teach As Jesus Did,* n. 136.

11. Henri Nouwen, *Creative Ministry* (New York: Doubleday, 1971), p. 116.

12. Briggs, *op. cit.,* p. 164.

13. *Ibid.,* pp. 171–172.

14. Strommen, *op. cit.,* p. 51.

2 | THE ADOLESCENT AS A HUMAN BEING

Before we can train young people to minister to their peers, it might be helpful to have some background information on the psychological makeup of this most fascinating and mysterious of all God's children.

The first point to keep in mind is the uniqueness of each young adult. We can't speak in terms of "adolescents," "teenagers," or "kids" as a general classification. Each one has his/her own gifts, talents, abilities, and personal story. Helping young people to see their individuality and to appreciate their unique nature is the task of the adult leader.

Anyone working with youth must be aware of their intrinsic goodness. Every young person is basically *good*. Repeat it over and over. Repeat it when they laugh at you. Repeat it when they come to your session with a fresh "high." Repeat it when you find chewing gum in the deep pile of your shag rug the next morning. Young adults are in a turbulent, pressure-filled period of their lives. They will do anything to ease the pain and hide their true feelings. They carry a multitude of masks, ready to be donned on any threatening situation. The louder and the more obnoxious an individual, the more pain he/she is covering.

As Eugene Kennedy says in *If You Really Knew Me, Would You Still Like Me?*:

> They wear masks they hope will cover up what they dislike about themselves. They harbor the strange hope that they will be liked for what they are. That includes the young girl who hides her naivete with super sophistication as well as the gangster who tries to look like a respectable suburbanite. Count in their numbers the weight lifter who hopes that his muscles will give him the manhood he inwardly questions. . . . These maneuvers to capture self-esteem make life resemble a pin-filled war map on which huge armies constantly circle for the best position.
>
> The great American pastime is not sports but the game of looking good and getting liked. The roots of its popularity are deep in the soil of our troubled self-esteem. Are we worth anything and how can we be sure?[1]

Kids are basically good but they try to hide their feelings of worthlessness in a variety of ingenious ways. This is an essential fact that should be imbedded in the minds of adult leaders. If not, they will be blown out of the room during the first meeting. The initial part of the peer ministry training program attempts to tear off the masks. Until they are removed, it is impossible to build self-esteem.

More than one good adult leader has left a training session berating "those rotten kids." They're not rotten—just misunderstood. To know them is to love them. And in order to love them, we have to understand them. What is beneath the masks of these mysterious creatures and how did they get so "messed up"?

DEVELOPMENTAL THEORY

One solution to the mystery is offered by the developmentalists, a group of psychological theorists who believe that human beings grow in stages. The concept is certainly not new to any parent who has uttered desperately, "I hope he's just going through a phase." The developmentalists have concretized and verbalized that which we have understood instinctively in the past. Developmental theory simply states that we travel through a series of distinct, well-defined stages on the road to personhood. These stages include our emotional, intellectual, moral, and faith development. In her book *Passages,* Gail Sheehy popularized one of the theories of adult emotional development.

There are some basic ground-rules for developmental stage theory. In most cases, stages are defined as a series of "cognitive reorganizations," each of which has "an identifiable shape, pattern and organization."[2] As one progresses along the ladder of stages, there is no turning back. He/she cannot revert to an earlier stage, although one may operate from different stages at different times. The individual proceeds from one stage to the next without skipping stages. The length of time one spends in a given stage will vary, but it is impossible to skip a stage. We operate out of our predominant stage only about 50% of the time and we should not stereotype young people at any time. As we mentioned before, each individual is unique and complex and cannot be reduced simply to a series of stages. We should expect any level to come forth from anyone at any time, even though we are operating from the basis of one predominant stage.

Those, in a nutshell, are the ground-rules of developmental stage theory. It is a simplistic presentation of a detailed system of personality development, but it will provide a foundation for our understanding of stages in growth, particularly as applied to the adolescent. In other words, where is he or she coming from?

EMOTIONAL DEVELOPMENT

We mentioned in the last chapter that Erik Erikson presented a theory of emotional growth characterized by eight crises. Each individual must face and resolve a crisis before proceeding to the next one. The eight crises and approximate corresponding ages are as follows:

1.	Trust vs. Mistrust	0 - 1
2.	Autonomy vs. Shame/Doubt	2 - 3
3.	Initiative vs. Guilt	4 - 6
4.	Industry vs. Inferiority	7 - 11
5.	Identity vs. Role Confusion	12 - 18
6.	Intimacy vs. Isolation	18 - 30
7.	Generativity vs. Stagnation	30 - 50
8.	Ego Identity vs. Despair	50 +

In the earliest stages of infancy a child must face the crisis of Trust vs. Mistrust. If he/she is held, picked up, and affectionately stroked, the infant will learn to trust others. On the other hand, if he/she is never held or stroked, but rather is constantly left to cry in the crib, the infant will trust no one and will travel through life as an emotional cripple. Autonomy vs. Shame/Doubt is a crisis familiar to all parents and relatives who have witnessed the "terrible twos." The child attempts to pull away from total dependence upon parents in the discovery that he/she is a separate human being. If the crisis of

24

Initiative vs. Guilt is resolved positively, the child enters that beautiful, helpful early school period when the refrigerator door is covered with color-and-paste "gifts" to mommy and daddy. The child who is encouraged and affirmed then resolves the Industry vs. Inferiority crisis by baking cookies, making model airplanes, and exploding holes in the hardwood floors with a special mixture from the chemistry set. In contrast, the young person who is "put down" continually during this crisis will, according to Erikson, develop an inferiority complex. As a teenager, the individual faces the crisis of Identity vs. Role Confusion as he/she tries to break away from family and traditional ties in order to establish an identity to truly call his/her own. Once the identity crisis is settled, the young adult searches for Intimacy and shuns Isolation. This is a time for intimate relationships and marriage to another human being or, in the case of the priest/religious, to God. Generativity vs. Stagnation is a crisis involving one's offspring as well as one's creative ideas and abilities. This is the period when many men and women wish to write a book, buy a house, or plant a tree in order to leave behind a little something of themselves when they go. The final crisis of Ego Identity vs. Despair is depicted best by walking into the neighborhood convalescent home. One look at the faces and postures of the residents will indicate those who have achieved an Ego Identity and those who have settled into a final state of Despair.

INTELLECTUAL STAGES

Swiss psychologist Jean Piaget outlined four stages of intellectual development that all of us must encounter. They are pictured thus:

1.	Sensorimotor	0 - 2
2.	Preoperational	2 - 7

During the Sensorimotor stage of intellectual development, the infant operates from a sense of motor activity. He/she learns to control hand movements and crawling techniques by *doing*. Stimulation in the child's environment, such as rattles or mobiles, can assist the progress of this stage. The pre-school child enters a whole new phase of thinking, so he/she colors, draws, works with shapes, and struggles with sizes. The Preoperational stage is characterized by concrete, literal thinking. Most pre-schoolers, shown two glasses containing equal amounts of water poured into a tall, thin beaker and a low, wide dish, will say that the beaker has more water than the dish. Reality is that which appears on the concrete level. In the Subperiod of Concrete Operations, the child's thinking begins to break out of the literal translation of the universe as abstract thinking evolves slowly into existence. The beaker experiment above will no longer fool the individual in this stage, yet he/she is still incapable of philosophical or theological explanation. At the time of early adolescence, however, the young person enters the period of Formal Operations and is able to think abstractly, theorize, idealize, and dream dreams with the best of us. The adolescent is fully capable of adult thinking and reasoning.

MORAL STAGES

Assuming we live long enough, all of us will apparently experience the crises and stages outlined above. In our moral development, however, most of us will only make it two-thirds of the way. That's the finding of the father of moral development, Lawrence Kohlberg, who illustrated six stages of progress in moral growth. They are:

1. Fear of Punishment
2. Ego Building
3. Good Boy/Nice Girl
4. Law and Order
5. Questioning the Reasons for Laws and Rules
6. Conscience and Principle

The terms above are simplified from such titles as the Instrumental Relativist Orientation and the Social-Contract Legalistic Orientation, and ages of moral development are difficult to pin down since people grow in this area at such a variety of speeds.

In the first stage, the child acts rightly out of a Fear of Punishment; he/she will not cross the street for fear of being spanked and sent to bed without supper. The second stage is characterized by "I'll scratch your back if you'll scratch mine." Ego Building is seen when the pre-schooler says that he/she will pick up the toys if there's a lollipop as a reward. The Good Boy/Nice Girl stage is that delightful period (alas, too short!) when the child behaves well to gain approval from authority. The little first-grader is good in church because he/she knows it pleases mommy and daddy. The fourth stage states that the law is uppermost and all law-breakers should be punished despite their reasons for breaking the law. The fifth stage questions the reason behind the law, and the sixth stage—one that very, very few individuals reach—operates upon the universal principles upon which laws are based.

FAITH STAGES

Using the research of Kohlberg's moral stages, James Fowler charted a series of six stages of faith development.

Again, to simplify Fowler's technical terms such as Individuating-Reflexive and Paradoxical-Consolidative, we will list them by the titles offered in Alfred McBride's *Creative Teaching in Christian Education:*[3]

1. Poet
2. Reasoner
3. Ecumenist
4. Personalizer
5. Tension-Bearer
6. Universalizer

The young child begins his/her journey in faith as a Poet who sees life in unified wholes. This is the simple belief that God, people, and the universe are all united. The youngster becomes a Reasoner when things become more complex, and he/she relies upon authority to resolve conflicts. His/her perceptions are very literal (e.g., God is an old man with a long beard who lives "up there" in heaven). The Ecumenist believes whatever the appropriate group believes. The group can be peers, friends, school or anyone who "counts." The Personalizer begins to break away from the group's beliefs and develop a personal faith, personal choices, and personal commitments. A few people move on to the Tension-Bearer stage in which they face up to the polarities before them and adopt a new respect for religious symbols and traditions. The very few who reach the stage of Universalizer live espoused principles such as love and justice; they get it all together and possess the simple faith of true believers; they are people, according to Fowler, like Jesus, Martin Luther King, and Malcolm X.

If these stages are too difficult to comprehend, John Westerhoff in *Will Our Children Have Faith?*[4] suggests four styles of faith. The first style, lasting from pre-school through early childhood, is Experienced Faith in which the child experiences the faith of others. He/she then moves on to Affiliative Faith (childhood to early adolescence) when he/she seeks to act with others in a community that has a strong identity. Searching Faith during adolescence and young adulthood is achieved when one begins to seriously question previous faith. Once the individual has searched he/she has the opportunity to attain an Owned Faith, a faith to call one's own and to share with anyone who will listen.

THE ADOLESCENT STAGE

Now that we have outlined the emotional, intellectual, moral, and faith stages of the individual, we would like to take a cross-section of these, slicing across the period of our lives known as adolescence. If we put all of the stages together correlating to their approximate age groups, we can observe an interesting portrait of the young adult.

By scanning the stages characteristic of the 12–18 group, we see that most young people are experiencing a severe identity crisis at the same time that their intellectual capacities are entering the stage of abstract thinking, while they are breaking away from a conformist approach to morality and searching for a faith of their own by reflecting upon the faith lives of others. No wonder adolescents appear to be off the wall much of the time!

Let's look at some of the implications of the above for those working with peer ministers. The junior or senior in high school is as intellectually capable of abstract reason as any adult, yet he/she is in emotional turmoil. The young person is down on himself/herself just at the time when our society expects such vital decisions as choosing a vocation and moving away from family and friends. Adult leaders of peer ministry can (and should!) talk to young people as adults, but must re-

AGE	EMOTIONAL	INTELLECTUAL	MORAL	FAITH	
0 - 1	Trust vs. Mistrust	Sensorimotor	Fear of Punishment		
2 - 3	Automony vs. Shame/Doubt	Preoperational	Ego Building		Experienced Faith
4 - 6	Initiative vs. Guilt		Good Boy/Nice Girl	Poet	
7 - 11	Industry vs. Inferiority	Subperiod of Concrete Operations	Law & Order	Reasoner	Affiliative Faith
12 - 18	Identity vs. Role Confusion	Formal Operations	Questioning Reasons	Ecumenist	Searching Faith
18 - 30	Intimacy vs. Isolation		Conscience & Principle	Personalizer	Owned Faith
30 - 50	Generativity vs. Stagnation			Tension-Bearer	
50 +	Ego Integrity vs. Despair			Universalizer	

spect the fact of their emotional tension. Thus, we try to work on points of feeling good about themselves and building self-esteem.

In addition to the emotional upset, their moral and faith development are entering a traumatic period of questioning and searching. For their entire lives, they have envisioned God as a concrete person living in the sky high above the clouds. Their moral response to life was sheltered by the security of laws and authority. Now, with grand new capacities of abstract thought, they begin to question a picture of God that doesn't make sense anymore and they search for new answers to the meaning of life and the existence of an Ultimate Being. They can't accept many laws that are promulgated from above, so they question the rationale behind them. The adult leader can facilitate these areas of search by providing an environment for open discussion and assisting the shake-up by prodding the young people with provocative questions. "In stage development, movement through the stages is effected when cognitive disequilibrium is created, that is, when a person's cognitive outlook is not adequate to cope with a given moral dilemma. . . . .When such a disequilibrium is provoked, it causes thinking about the inadequacies of one's reasons and a search for better and more adequate reasons."[5]

This is the method of peer ministry training. Provide an environment for open discussion during weekly sessions or weekend retreats. Then break down the walls of low self-esteem and assist their search for a new faith in Jesus Christ. As these young people open up and put on Christ, they will go into the marketplace and share their owned faith with their peers.

NOTES

1. Eugene Kennedy, *If You Really Knew Me, Would You Still Like Me?* (Niles, Ill.: Argus, 1975), p. 12.

2. Ronald Duska and Mariellen Whelan, *Moral Development: A Guide to Piaget and Kohlberg* (New York: Paulist, 1975), p. 6.

3. New York: Seabury, 1976.

4. Boston: Allyn and Bacon, 1978.

5. Duska and Whelan, *op. cit.,* p. 49.

3 | PEER MINISTRY TRAINING PROGRAM

THE GROUP

The peer ministry group is a group unto itself which meets and then disperses to work with other groups. The following five rules for groups should always be observed.

1. Confidentiality is a vital part of the group meeting. It is necessary to tell younger people that what is said within the group is to stay within the group.

2. Sharing is essential for group success. The sharing of feelings—both positive and negative—is much more important than the sharing of opinions and ideas.

3. Each person speaking in the group needs the attention and support of all other members of the group. Support cannot be presumed unless it is expressed.

4. Confrontation of others' shortcomings can be appropriate within the group if feelings are expressed with gentleness and care. Groups are not places to hold arguments, however.

5. When speaking in a group speak about yourself, speak for yourself, and refer to yourself as "I."

THE INITIAL LEADERS' WORKSHOP
FOR PEER MINISTRY TRAINING

All of these exercises are to be done in one group. There should be a maximum of twelve peer ministers and two adult group leaders.

Each group leader should read and study the program carefully in advance. Please note necessary materials and gather them before the program begins.

8:00 P.M. Warm-up exercises—if someone plays a guitar, people might sing along or you can play "Simon Says" or use "Crowd Breakers" from Lyman Coleman's *Encyclopedia of Serendipity* (Serendipity House, 1976).

8:30 P.M. Materials needed: A small paper bag containing various similar kinds of unrelated materials such as paper clips, a paper cup, string, pipe cleaners, etc.

Ask all members of the group to be as creative as possible and to construct a symbol of themselves as they see themselves at this point in personal history. After construction of the symbols, have each member share his or hers and explain the symbol to the group. In this and in all exercises, the adult leaders should participate as much as the peer minister.

9:30 P.M. Pair the members of the group in twos and have each pair go to a private place and share with each other his or her greatest fear about being a peer minister or the greatest weakness which he or she feels will be a detriment to his or her work.

9:45 P.M. Break

10:00 P.M.   Materials needed: Paper and crayons.
             Each person should have a piece of paper and cray-
             ons. Ask the participants to color a symbol of how
             they have changed in the past two years. After every-
             one has drawn his or her symbol, share them with the
             group.

11:00 P.M.   End the evening with a candlelight shared prayer
             meeting.

THE NEXT DAY

9:00 A.M.   Begin the day with more warm-up exercises.

9:30 A.M.   Materials needed: Paper and pencils.
             Give each member of the group a piece of paper and a
             pencil. Ask the participants to share first on paper and
             then in the group all of the things which they feel they
             could never do in life (e.g., talk in front of a group of
             people, change a flat tire, dissect a frog in school, etc.).
             Discuss in the group the difference between saying "I
             can't do something" and "I won't do something." This
             analysis between "can't" and "won't" can open the
             door of self-discovery of new potential within us.

10:30 A.M.   Break

10:45 A.M.   Materials needed: Paper and pencils.
             On a piece of paper have the participants write down
             all of the strengths which they think they possess. Ask
             them to share these aloud with their group.

11:30 A.M.   Materials needed: Everyone's name in a hat.
             Have each member of the group draw the name of an-

other member out of a hat. Take the name received and after a moment or two of thought tell that person aloud within the group all the strengths that you perceive in him or her and how you feel he or she will contribute to peer ministry.

12:00 P.M.   Lunch and relax

1:30 P.M.   Discuss with the group at some length the five ground-rules for group process as found at the beginning of this chapter.

2:00 P.M.   Materials needed: Paper and pencil.
Each group member should write down three sentences listing three areas in which he or she feels need of help at this time in life. This exercise should be done deliberately and thoughtfully. Then ask each member of the group to share at least one of those areas with the entire group. The length of time that this exercise will take depends upon the size of the group. The leader should be sure that everyone has spoken before the group ends. After an hour and a half, a break should be taken. For a group of eight, three hours will probably be necessary; for a group of twelve, four and a half hours.

Closing: A meal together is an appropriate way to end this workshop.

MEETINGS

Peer ministry groups need three kinds of meetings:

1. programming
2. personal growth sharing
3. educational workshops

By programming, we refer to all the experiences that peer ministers will plan and provide for younger people. Planning can be a long and tedious process, and this is a hard lesson for some peer ministers to learn. If the peer ministers were planning the sample retreat found in this chapter, it would be decided who would give which talk, who would be leading various exercises within the small groups, and who would be responsible for materials and other practical details.

PERSONAL GROWTH MEETINGS

In addition to the initial workshop peer ministers need a monthly meeting with an open space of time for at least two hours where those in the group can share any concerns they wish. Some of these concerns may revolve around feelings about experiences functioning as a peer minister. Or it may happen individuals may simply wish to talk about themselves and some problems that they are currently experiencing with life. At this type of meeting the members are ministering not to younger people but to one another, and this is a very important aspect of their task. It should be remembered that the peer ministry group itself is both a miniature of the Church as well as a training laboratory for working groups with younger people. Much can be learned in these experiences of deep personal sharing. They can provide the opportunity for a lot of healing and human growth. At least one adult who is somewhat skilled in group process should be consistently present as the leader of this monthly meeting. Occasionally, it is good to take a longer stretch of time such as a Sunday afternoon for these meetings and to combine them with a social activity like a candlelight spaghetti supper or going out together after the meeting for pizza. A group liturgy or a para-liturgy can be very appropriate also at these times.

EDUCATIONAL WORKSHOP

Periodically, it is good for peer ministers to have formal training in areas that will directly help them in their work such as communicating skills, public speaking, and group dynamics. There are often many professional resource people within the community who are only too happy to assist in the training of youth. On the following pages are several exercises which can be used very effectively in the education of peer ministers.

1. Communication and Position Change
(Excerpted from *Designs in Affective Education* by Elizabeth W. Flynn and John F. LaFaso, Paulist Press, 1974.)

Purpose: To examine the discussion behavior of a group as it is affected by changes in physical positioning.

Comment: When other variables in the physical environment are held constant, but group members change their "seating" arrangements so that individual position, spatial relationships and physical position in the group change, noticeable changes may occur in such group operations as participation patterns, communication level, procedure, norms and content of the discussion.

Group Size: 5–15. May be used with a larger group if assistant leadership is available for subgrouping.

Time Suggested: One to two hours.

General Directions: This exercise may be introduced unexpectedly or may be planned for by the group if additional materials are needed. It may be introduced early in a group's life, and may be used as one of their experiences in "process discussion."

The particular changes to be made and the times at which they are to be made should be selected by the leader. It is possible that group members may begin to make other suggested changes, and these should be accepted if possible, but the pace at which changes are made should not be increased. After each of these changes, or after several of them, the group should shift temporarily to a "process discussion" (see Step No. 3) and talk about what effects, if any, their change in position made on their group and its discussion.

Materials Required: More floor space may be required for this exercise than is normally occupied by the group, but by pushing unused furniture to the walls most rooms will be quite adequate. In addition to the usual chairs, which must be movable, a reasonably clean rug or carpet will help. If this is not available, the floor area to be used may be swept clean before the group meets.

Discussion Materials: The discussion content may be based on an issue, problem or subject which arose in a previous discussion and proved to be of interest, but for which time for adequate exploration was not available. A new topic of known interest may be used for which the group has had some preparation or for which a brief presentation has been made at the beginning of the session prior to the start of the exercise. If necessary, it is possible for the group members to have a book or paper in their hands during most, but not all, of this discussion time. A discussion in which frequent reference must be made to projected slides, chalkboard materials, or posted or displayed material would not be suitable.

Procedure:

1. The group starts discussing a topic of general interest seated in the usual way, with the leader seated among them, facilitating the discussion by his questions.

2. After discussing for 10–15 minutes, the leader recommends a change in position, moving himself into the new situation. Changes should be made as quickly and easily as possible, and the new position tried for another 10–15 minutes to allow any possible effects to be noticed. The following possibilities may be tried:

- a group which normally sits in chairs around a table may abandon the table, but remain seated in the same positions
- a group seated in chairs may stand in the same locations in which they have been sitting
- the group may move and sit on the floor in the same relative position
- the group may sit on the floor spacing themselves farther apart or closer together
- the group may stand, pushing close together so that shoulders are touching
- the group may stand facing outward, in a tight circle with backs touching
- the group may kneel, facing each other
- the kneeling group may pull in closer, placing their hands on one another's shoulders, or holding hands
- the group, seated on the floor, may face outward, sitting back to back in a tight circle
- the group may lie prone, forming the spokes of a wheel, with their heads close together

3. After each of these changes, or after several of them, the group should shift to process discussion. The leader may assist the group with questions such as the following:

- Which position tried seemed to elicit the most laughter? Why?
- Which position seemed to provide the "best" discussion? Why?
- Did some people talk more than usual this time? Less than usual? Why?
- Did some people refuse to change their position? Why?

How did the rest of the group accept this? Why?
- Was there a change in "who talks to whom"? Why?

4. The leader may find that his own tendency will be to change his style or manner of leadership in some way as he moves with the group. He, too, should reflect on the experience and express his feelings and ideas as to what he notices about this and why this happened.

5. If desired, the discussion may be continued by thinking about other "discussion" situations in the broad sense of the term, and how they are affected by seating arrangements, physical arrangement of the group, and physical positioning of the leader in relation to the group.

Variations:

1. One or two members may be asked to serve the group as observers, remaining outside the group during the discussion proper, and rejoining it during the "process discussions." Particularly in a "new" group, observers should be asked to make general observations about the group and "what happened," without referring to people by name.

2. Instead of performing all the variations on the basis of a circle pattern, single or multiple row patterns may be introduced, with many of the above variations introduced.

2. Listening

(Excerpted from *Awareness Experiences for School Use* by Bette Hamlin, Pflaum Publishing, 1975)

The Idea: Really hearing what another person expresses is a basic skill in communication. True listening involves more than just hearing words and content. It includes hearing meanings and feelings. When you hear what a person says, means, and feels, then he feels validated. When his identity is validated, he is in a better position to solve his problems. Something also happens to the listener when he really hears. He becomes more aware of the speaker and also aware of his own bias. The skill is also helpful in settling differences and clarifying thoughts and feelings.

The Activity:
1. Explain that:

- A sender sends a message to the receiver.
- An observer notices how the message is sent and may offer helpful suggestions.
- Just because the message is sent does not mean that it was heard or understood.

2. Arrange the class in dyads (with a sender and a receiver), or in triads (with an observer added).

3. Each person in the group takes a turn being a sender and a receiver (and an observer, if in a triad).

The sender sends a message starting with "I" (a statement, not a question).

The receiver tries to get the sender to respond "Yes" to these questions:

a. "Did I hear you say (repeat what you heard him say) . . . ?"
b. "Do you mean . . . ?"
c. "Do you mean . . . ?"

If the sender responds with "Yes" or agrees with a nod, etc., the receiver goes to the next question. If the sender responds with "No" or "Partly," the sender must give more information to clarify his first statement.

4. "What did you experience when someone heard what

44

you said?" "What did you experience when you listened carefully and checked out meanings?"

Encourage the receiver to feed back real meanings and perceptions, not just repetitious words or self-biases. For example:

Sender:	"I'm afraid to walk home."
Receiver:	"Did I hear you say that you are afraid to walk home?"
Sender:	"Yes."
Receiver:	"Do you mean you are afraid to walk home?" (repetitious)
Receiver:	"Do you mean you're afraid you'll be late for the rehearsal if you take the time to walk home for dinner?" (checking the meaning)
Sender:	"Yes."

3. Role and Reversal

(Excerpted from *Awareness: Exploring Experimenting Experiencing* by John O. Stevens, Real People Press, 1971)

I want the group to decide on a specific role that fits each individual in the group. Focus on one person at a time and quickly get several suggestions for a role that expresses one way this person impresses you. Realize that there are many possibilities for roles. When you have decided on an appropriate role for this person, go on to make this role more specific and detailed. If you have decided on the role of nurse, go on to describe what kind of nurse the person is. Is this person a tough, strong, no-nonsense nurse or a cheerful young candy-striper? After you have done this, decide on a simple sentence that would be appropriate for this person to say in this role. For my nurse example, an appropriate sentence might be "Cheer up now; this won't hurt a bit and you'll be well in no time." Now decide on these roles and sentences for everyone in the group, and be sure that each person understands exactly what role and sentence he or she has been given.

Now that we each have our roles and sentences, I want us all to play these roles for the next eight minutes. Really invest yourself in this role and interact with the others in the group in whatever way is appropriate for this role. As you interact with others, alternate saying this given sentence with saying any other sentence you want to.

Now stop and absorb your experience of doing this. How did you feel in your role, and what did you notice about yourself and others as you did this? Now take about five minutes to share your experience of playing this role.

Now take a few minutes to realize what the exact opposite of your role and your sentence could be. For instance, the reverse of a young candy-striper nurse whose sentence is "Cheer up now; this won't hurt a bit and you'll be well in no time," is an old patient who groans "Ohhh, this is going to hurt and I'll be sick for a long time." You might want some help from others in your group to decide on the exact opposite of your role and sentence.

Now that we all have our opposite roles and sentences, I want us all to play these roles for the next eight minutes. Really invest yourself in your role, and interact with others in the group in whatever way is appropriate for this role. As you interact with others, alternate saying this opposite sentence with saying any other sentence you want to.

Now stop and absorb what you experienced while playing this reverse role. How did you feel in this role, and what did you become aware of as you did this? Which role was easiest for you to play, your original role or the reverse? What did you notice about others as they did this? Now take five or ten minutes to share your experiences and your observations with each other.

Now I want all of you to switch back and forth between

your original role and its reverse. As you interact with others, play one role for about twenty seconds, and then switch quickly to the reverse. Do this for about eight minutes.

Again share your experience of doing this.

(This experiment can also be very useful if you ask each individual to choose his or her own detailed role and short sentence instead of having the group decide.)

4. Learning to Listen
(Excerpted from *Peer Program For Youth* by Ardyth Hebeisen, Augsburg Publishing House, 1973)

Purpose: to provide a base sharing experience between two people before learning special communication skills.

Ask each person in the group to find a partner—someone he or she hasn't seen much of lately. Each person in the pair will have about five minutes to tell his or her partner about something that has been very exciting, or troubling, but something that he or she has strong feelings about.

When the time is up, call the group together again and move on to the mini-lecture. The group will discuss this experience at the end of the session.

(a) Mini-Lecture: Introduction to Reflective Listening
Purpose: to provide a context for trying reflective listening; to describe conceptually what reflective listening is.

Before you present this material to the group it is important for you to really know and understand it. This is a verbatim demonstration of what might be said to teach the concept of reflective listening:

> Throughout this series we have been working on learning our relationships. We have been experiencing more and more understanding and acceptance. Now we would like to turn our attention to learning the communication skills

47

that make it possible to talk directly about the under-standing we are reaching for. Suppose you are talking with a person who has a lot of feelings. Maybe he is upset about something—or feels especially good. How can you communicate acceptance of what he is saying so he will feel encouraged to continue to share with you? You can do it through reflective listening, which looks like this:

Your friend has expressed his feelings, or described something to you. To make sure you understand him, or to show your acceptance of what you understand him to say, you say to him, in different words, what you under-stand him to mean. You provide a kind of mirror or re-flection of what he is saying.

If he says, "I'm so sick I can hardly stand up," you might respond, "Wow, you're really feeling rotten." If he says, "Hey, guess what! I made the first team in swimming," you might say, "The first team! You really sound excit-ed."

The main thing you want to hear and respond to when people share in this way is their feeling. If your response can pick up and reflect feelings, you are closer to what is going on inside the other person, and your communication is more true and more close to what's really happening. Sometimes what you feed back to the other person is a kind of summarizing, like, "So the teacher blamed you for something Tom did, and now you've been criticized and you don't want to tell her what really happened because you don't want to sell out on Tom." Sometimes this is also very helpful in communicating understanding and helping the other person clarify his own situation. The important key in reflective listening is to listen as accurately as possible to what the other person is saying—and to send this meaning back to him in different words. Your response is based on the other person's feelings. Your goal is to be in touch with what is happening inside him.

(b) Demonstration of Reflective Listening

Purpose: to provide a model to demonstrate reflective listening

Ask a volunteer from the group to think of some problem he has right now—perhaps a teacher he is having trouble with, or a friend who irritates him, or a decision he has to make. Ask him to tell the group about it, and let them respond in whatever ways seem natural to them. Ask the problem-sharer to stop talking after each sentence or two, so that the group has time to respond.

Now ask the problem-sharer to begin again, and to tell the same problem to the leader, while the group merely listens. This time the leader tries to reflect the feelings and/or content of what the sharer is saying.

Discuss what different things happened in the two situations. Were the two conversations different in tone? Were they different in what subjects were discussed, or how they were discussed? How does the problem-sharer feel about the two conversations? If it seems useful, you might try the same exercise again with a different problem-sharer and a different problem.

5. Active Listening
(Excerpted from *Peer Program For Youth* by Ardyth Hebeisen, Augsburg Publishing House, 1973)

(a) Reflective Listening Responses

Purpose: to provide another experience in intensive use of reflective listening responses

Explain to the group that you'll be doing quick reviews of both reflective listening and "I" messages and then focusing on some role-play situations where they will have an opportunity to use both skills.

Suggest that each person find a partner with whom he has not yet practiced reflective listening. In the pairs, spend five minutes each talking about something that happened during the week that each one has a lot of feelings about. The listening partner should do reflective listening.

(b) Practice of "I" Messages

Purpose: to review the "I" message, and to provide practice using an "I" message in varied situations which will arouse positive or negative responses

Give a quick review of the "I" message and the three parts: what happened, how I feel, and how this affects me.

Using the "I" Message Practice Sheet, present these situations to members of the group and ask them to respond with the kind of "I" message they would give if they were in that situation. Coach the group members where they need it as they work to develop greater skill in communicating their feelings. Point out:

> "I" messages can be used as a way of helping other people change their behavior. If they are unaware of what it is in their own behavior that tends to get them in trouble with other people, your honest response to them through a straight "I" message is one of the most effective ways of helping them to know and to change their own behavior.

"I" MESSAGE PRACTICE SHEET

What "I" messages would you send to these?

1. Your new friend seems to like going places with you, but he is always late. You have to wait at least

a half hour for him every time you do something together. Often you are late getting to ballgames or
movies. Tonight he picks you up at your house. He
is forty-five minutes late.

2. You've been trying to be a friend to Sally, but she
has latched on and wants to be with you all the
time. You don't get the time you want to be with
other friends, have time alone, and just do your
own thing.

3. You've found a friend (opposite sex) whom you
really would like to help and be friends with, but he
or she keeps putting on a big sex come-on.

4. Your friend has been changing gradually. The
clothes he wears have been getting way-out. You
have noticed that you are becoming embarrassed
when you go places with him.

5. You come home to find that your roommate (sister,
brother) has just cleaned the room you share. He's
there, and you say . . .

6. Your friend has just called at 11:30 P.M. You were
in bed sleeping. He says, ''Hi. I just thought I'd call
and rap for a while.''

7. You've been out of touch with your friend for a
while. You've really missed him—but you've been
busy. Now you go to the store to pick up some
things, and you run across him there.

8. You are goofing around with some kids. One of
them takes some goopy stuff and drips it over your
clothes.

9. You have a new friend. Today you found him or her
flirting with your steady.

10. Your mom cooked a supper of some of your favorite foods.

11. You're housebound with a broken leg. Your friend
gives up the ballgame and dance and spends the
evening keeping you company.

12. You're taking a test. Your classmate keeps trying to read your answers over your shoulder.

13. Your new friend borrowed your favorite sweater to wear to a party. When he or she returns it, it is dirty and there's a small hole in the elbow. He or she says nothing about it and acts as though nothing has happened.

6. Role Play

(Excerpted from *Designs in Affective Education* by Elizabeth W. Flynn and John F. LaFaso, Paulist Press, 1974)

1. Select two role players and instruct them separately and secretly. The situation: two people meet and engage in a conversation. The roles: "A"—relaxed and comfortable, but eager to tell the other an experience he has had recently. "B"—has another engagement and is eager to get away quickly, but tries to be polite and to give the appearance of interested listening, while not mentioning the fact that he must leave or he will be late for his appointment. Be sure "A" knows what engagement he is hurrying toward—they need not tell you, but must be clear about this themselves before they start. In this case they are to talk—this is not a non-verbal, but a para-verbal experiment.

2. Explain to the "audience" that they are to look for para-verbal clues in the following role play. Tell them the situation, but not the roles.

3. Allow the role play to run 3–5 minutes, until some frustration or irritation becomes obvious.

4. Start the general discussion of the experience by asking the role players how they felt in their roles. Ask them to tell the group their roles.

• How did "B's" muscles feel? How does he feel now? Can he recreate the muscular sensations he felt then?

- Was "A" aware of his partner's eagerness to leave? How did he feel about this? How did his muscles feel? Did he believe "B" was "really listening" to him? What did he notice about his own physical behavior?
- What did the observers notice about the gestures and facial expressions of the role players? How did they think the role players were feeling? What clues made them think this?

If desired, following this or other parts of the exercise, the students may make individual lists of the ways in which we communicate non-verbally. They may share these lists in sub-groups and discuss ways in which we encourage or discourage others by non-verbal communication. Ask them to think about the kinds of non-verbal communication that accompany words (para-verbal or para-linguistic communication) and the kinds we act out without words. Are there some things which can be better expressed verbally? Some which are better expressed non-verbally? Some which require both? Is there really such a thing as verbal expression without non-verbal or para-verbal accompaniment? Does the non-verbal accompany the verbal, or does the verbal accompany the non-verbal?

Variation: To try to experience ways to communicate feelings.

1. Divide the class in half. Form two rows facing one another across the room.

2. Ask the students to begin moving very slowly toward someone. Tell them that when they are aware of a clear feeling they are to express it in a movement or posture, e.g., hold their head in their hands, dance, jump. Tell the students it is important to keep all expressions as authentic or genuine as possible.

3. Tell the students, "If you are approached, you may respond cooperatively or antagonistically, or even ignore the person and walk away. Do not 'play-act.' "

4. After 10–15 minutes, seat the group to discuss "what happened."

SPIRITUAL FORMATION

Peer ministry groups are in need of continuing spiritual formation. One suggestion is to close each peer meeting with a short candlelight prayer service. In this context, many concerns of people are brought to the surface. On personal growth days the groups meeting can be followed by a liturgy or a para-liturgy or a prayer service. Spiritual nourishment is as vital to youth as to adults. Involvement in the liturgical life of the parish or school is another source of formation. For youth themselves, we recommend *Getting in Touch with Jesus* by Joseph Moore, Liguori Publications, 1980, a good spiritual guide book for young people. For help to the youth minister in giving spiritual direction to young people, we recommend "Counselling The Teenager," *The Living Light,* Vol. 14, No. 4, Winter, 1977, pages 563–574.

There are two religious movements today where teenagers can be ministered to by young adults in the fostering of a personal spirituality. One is called "Young Life" and is born out of the evangelical Protestant tradition. In various parts of the United States, summer camps are held for teenagers for varying lengths of time. For further information write: Young Life, 720 W. Monument St., P.O. Box 520 Colorado Springs, Col. 80901.

Another growing movement and closer to the Roman Catholic tradition is "Taize." Taize, an ecumenical monastery in southeastern France, has become a center for Christian religious revival in Europe among young adults. Especially in the summertime, a few thousand youth are at Taize for a week or month of intense prayer and discussion. The contemplative life is very obvious among these youth as is a global concern for social justice. Taize is not appropriately called a "movement" because there is constant encouragement from the Brothers of Taize to have the young people return to their own churches to bring them a new vitality.

For any teenager able to afford it, a week at Taize in France is well worth the time and money. Taize is about a three and a half hour train ride from Paris, and housing (large tents) and on-campus food service is nominal (about $5 per diem for North Americans). However there are also Taize-associated prayer groups now in the United States, particularly along the East coast. For further information write: Taize Community, 413 W. 48th St., New York, N.Y. 10036. Also recommended from France is the newsletter (English version) Write: Taize Communaute, 71250, Taize, France (send $10 by check drawn on a French bank).

Some of the data previously quoted in the handbook indicates that while religious fervor among young adults is widespread, Church attendance declines. Part of the reason for this phenomenon is that the community which the Church should be is not a reality for many youth. Peer ministry offers at least one context where the desire to help others and a spiritual hunger for God can be concretized in the here and now. This is crucial in the spiritual development of teenagers. They need to feel, at a deep level, that they are very much members of the parish community. Awareness of their own capacity for ministry is very helpful toward this end. So often it can seem to the young that involvement in and service to the Church is adult business. And adults reinforce this feeling if they fail to provide meaningful ways for the young to be members of the community—not token members, but *real* members. Thus we see the spiritual quest of young people today being nourished and matured *within* the community when provided with structured opportunities to minister.

INTRODUCTION TO TRAINING SESSIONS

It is important to have a preparation period preceding the commissioning of the youth ministers. There are two major reasons for this. First of all, it allows the young people time to get to know each other better, form a group for mutual support, and establish a corporate identity. Second, it enables the adult trainers time and a process to screen the applicants. It may be that some candidate has just too many life problems to be able to serve others at this point; it may also be that someone who is a real hindrance to the effective functioning of the group will be observed. The training sessions provide a legitimate and fair process for determining which candidates will be accepted as peer ministers.

Finally, let us remark that the sessions are educational in themselves, helping the young people to grow both in self-knowledge and the dynamics of group interaction that are so important in their future work in peer ministry.

NOTES TO FACILITATORS OF TRAINING SESSIONS

The following are suggested time-frames per session based on a group of ten people (Time may vary depending on how verbal participants are.)

Session I. 45 minutes. Background instrumental music is helpful during this session. Save "Me" posters for use in Session XIII.

Session II. 1½ hours. Discuss the profile with the group upon completion.

Session III. 2 hours. Discuss the familygram with the group upon completion.

Session IV. 20 minutes. Score the questionnaire privately and return to participants. Anyone with five (or more) "F's" has definite *leadership potential. (Three "O's" = one "F".)*

Session V. 1½ hours. This exercise is a deeper probe of an exercise during the Initial Workshop. Discuss the probe with the group upon completion.

Session VI. 1 hour. Discuss the paragraph with the group upon completion. Save baby pictures for use in Session XIII.

Session VII. 1 hour, 15 minutes. Be sure to point out the "cross" as a concrete daily reality *already* present in each life.

Session VIII. 1 hour. Discuss the index with the group upon completion.

Session IX. 1 hour, 15 minutes. Discuss the sheet with the group upon completion. Be sure to point out that feelings in themselves are neither bad nor good, right nor wrong. Morality comes into play only in the response of our behavior to our feelings. For our actions we are responsible.

Session X. 2 hours. Discuss the sheet with the group upon completion.

Session XI. 1 hour. Discuss the sheet with the group upon completion.

Session XII. 1 hour. (May be a good preliminary to the prayer service.)

Session XIII. 1 hour.

GROUND RULES FOR THE INITIAL WORKSHOP AND THE TRAINING SESSIONS

It is important to follow some basic rules to enhance any group meeting.

1. Meet in a room or space that is comfortable and informal. Atmosphere is very important. Dim lighting is advisable; also a burning candle in the center of the group symbolizes the sacredness of the occasion.

2. Sit *close together*. Physical closeness is extremely helpful. Also everyone should be able to see *the face* of each person in the group.

3. Speak in the first person using "I" (*not* the second person "you").

TIME-FRAMES FOR THE SESSIONS

The training sessions can be pieced together in various ways according to your preference. We suggest these two options.

Option 1. An intense weekend experience, perhaps in late summer just before the academic year.

Option 2. On a weekly *or* bi-weekly basis, perhaps in the summer *or* semester immediately preceding actual ministry.

Important Note: If you are within a Catholic high school:

- Do not meet in a classroom unless the atmosphere is informal.
- Meet outside the school day and the perimeters imposed by class-time lengths.

If discussions during *any* of the sessions run ninety minutes, it is best to take a break for fifteen minutes and then return.

INTRODUCTION TO THE INITIAL WORKSHOP AND TRAINING SESSIONS

(For the *initial workshop* to be effective it is necessary that it be contained within one twenty-four hour time frame.)

These two experiences begin your formation as a peer minister. They have much to offer you individually as well as the entire group as a group. Please consider the following before you begin.

1. You must be willing to open up yourself and share in the group. Very soon you will be in a position where you will be asking this of others. You will have no right to ask others to risk and grow if you have not risked and grown yourself.

2. Be observant of adult leaders. Try to learn skills by watching others more experienced than you.

3. Enjoy the inward focus that these experiences will give you. Delight in the new things you learn about yourself and the deeper bonds you make with others. *However,* never forget that this turning inward is only a part of peer ministry. But it is not the essence. You will soon be called upon after your training to look *outward* and help new people to grow.

4. When you talk in a group, be careful not to become philosophical (which is often escapism). Be as *personal* as possible.

SESSION I: THE "ME SHEET"

Materials: poster paper and crayons/masking tape on a large poster

Complete the "Me Sheet." When all are finished, tape your poster to your chest. Walk about the room in silence reading each other's sheets. *Be sure* to go to everyone in the group. When you are finished be seated and wait for the others. Save the "Me" posters for use in Session XIII.

"ME SHEET"

POSSIBLE
CAREER
INTEREST

THREE
ADJECTIVES
TO DESCRIBE
YOUR PERSONALITY

NAME YOU LIKE TO BE CALLED

PLACES YOU HAVE LIVED

THREE
FAVORITE
PASTIMES

"SONG" TITLE
WHICH BEST DESCRIBES
YOUR PHILOSOPHY
OF LIFE

SESSION II: STRENGTH PROFILE

Strengths of My Personality		Weaknesses in My Personality	
1.	———	1.	———
2.	———	2.	———
3.	———	3.	———
4.	———	4.	———
5.	———	5.	———
6.	———	6.	———
7.	———	7.	———
8.	———	8.	———
9.	———	9.	———
10.	———	10.	———

Put the following letter after the strength or weakness which you may feel is related to it by virtue of inheritance or influence.

D - my Dad
M - my Mom
B - my Brother
S - my Sister
G - my Grandparent
N - my Nationality
E - my Environment
T - my Training, Upbringing, Schooling
F - my Friends

SESSION III: FAMILYGRAM

Draw a diagram of yourself in relationship with your immediate family. Physical closeness and distance in the diagram should indicate psychological closeness and distance.

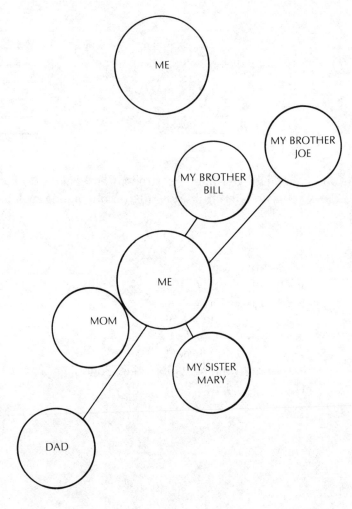

SESSION IV: LEADERSHIP QUESTIONNAIRE

Directions: The following items describe aspects of leadership behavior. Respond to each item according to the way you would most likely act. Circle whether you would most likely behave in the described situation always (A), frequently (F), occasionally (O), seldom (S), or never (N).

A F O S N   (1) I allow other people to work in a group in the manner of their choosing; I respect freedom of action.

A F O S N   (2) I usually stay to clean up.

A F O S N   (3) I have worked on a group project.

A F O S N   (4) I enjoy positions of authority in a group.

A F O S N   (5) I schedule my homework pretty much.

A F O S N   (6) I have run for a class or club office.

A F O S N   (7) I enjoy making persuasive arguments.

A F O S N   (8) I notice that others sometimes follow my influence.

A F O S N   (9) I'm quiet, but when I speak, people listen carefully.

A F O S N   (10) I find that people try to get to know me better.

A F O S N   (11) I like to express my own ideas in a group.

A F O S N   (12) I like to operate at the maximum of my potential.

A F O S N   (13) I enjoy competitive sports and/or games.

A F O S N   (14) When involved in a group project, I feel personally responsible for the results.

A F O S N   (15) I'm open to trying new things and ideas. People tell me that they see me as a strong person.

SESSION V: WEAKNESS PROBE

Very often when we say "I can't" we really mean "I won't." Test your honesty about your *real* weaknesses as opposed to your *imagined* ones by trying to complete this page as best you can.

When I say "I can't . . ."   What I really mean is . . .
1.   1.
2.   2.
3.   3.
4.   4.
5.   5.

SESSION VI: BAPTISM TODAY

Keeping a picture of yourself as a baby in front of you, write a paragraph about what it *now* means to you to be a baptized Christian. How have your views changed and grown since your own baptism?

Note: save the baby picture for use in Session XIII.

SESSION VII: CROSSROADS

1. Listen to the Scripture reading: Luke 9:23–25.
2. Listen to the song "Follow Me" (from the album *Take Me to Tomorrow*, R.C.A. Victor, 1970).

Answer: What does it mean in *your* personal life to take up the cross each day? Share your thoughts with the group.

SESSION VIII: PRAYER INDEX

Frequency:

I pray:_____ per day

_____ per week

_____ per month

Form:

My favorite form of prayer is:_____

_____

_____

_____

Difficulty:

My major difficulty in praying is:_____

_____

_____

_____

Place:

The place I like to pray is:_____

_____

_____

_____

SESSION IX: FEELINGS

Two feelings I experience which I wish I didn't have:
1.
2.

I usually cope with these feelings by:
1.
2.

I wish I could cope with these feelings in the future by:
1.
2.

SESSION X: GROWTH SHEET

Complete the following.

A recent trouble I have had which has helped me to grow:

_____

_____

_____

Two areas in my life in which I feel I need help in order to grow.

1._____

_____

_____

_____

2._____

_____

_____

_____

SESSION XI: MINISTRY MANDATE

Listen to the Scripture Reading, Mark 16:14–18, and answer the following:

Some ways I see myself "going forth" into the world:

_____

_____

_____

Some ways I can see myself ministering to my peers:

_____

_____

_____

SESSION XII: THE VELVETEEN RABBIT

Read the following reflectively. Then discuss with the group what it means for *you* to be real and what difficulties *you* encounter in that process.

"Real isn't how you are made," said the Skin Horse. "It's a thing that happens to you when a child loves you for a long, long time, not just to play with, but REALLY loves you. Then you become Real."

"Does it hurt?" asked the Rabbit.

"Sometimes," said the Skin Horse, for he was always truthful. "When you are Real you don't mind being hurt."

"Does it happen all at once, like being wound up," he asked, "or bit by bit?"

"It doesn't happen all at once," said the Skin Horse. "You become. It takes a long time. That's why it doesn't often happen to people who break easily, or have sharp edges, or who have to be carefully kept. Generally by the time you are Real, most of your hair has been loved off, and your eyes drop out and you get loose in the joints and very shabby. But these things don't matter at all, because once you are Real you can't be ugly, except to people who don't understand."

SESSION XIII: PRAYER SESSION

Hang the "Me" posters from Session I and the baby pictures from Session VI around the room for prayer. The group should sit in a circle on the floor with a crucifix in the middle next to a lighted candle.

1. Open with the song "Follow Me" (from Session VII).
2. Someone should read aloud the Scripture passage Luke 9:23–25.
3. Pass around the crucifix. Each person should take it and look at the corpus of Jesus and say a prayer either aloud or silently.
4. Spend some minutes in quiet group contemplation.
5. Conclude with a song or hymn familiar to all in the group.

SAMPLE PERSONAL GROWTH RETREAT

The following is a twenty-four hour experience which can be used successfully with underclassmen and teamed by peer ministers once peer ministers themselves have experienced it with their adult leaders.

Each retreat leader should read and study the program carefully in advance. Please note necessary materials and gather them before the program begins.

7:00 P.M.   Large Group - "Welcome" - Leader: _____.
A peer minister introduces the overnight experience and reviews the ground-rules of the group process with the young people. He or she sets the tone for the evening which should be both serious and happy.

7:15 P.M.   Large Group - "Warm-Up" - Leader: _____.
Have the group make an outer circle and an inner circle facing each other. The leader will announce to

each pair an item to be discussed between them for 30–60 seconds. When the leader blows his whistle to signal that the time is ended, everyone on the outer circle takes one step to the right to face a new person while the inner circle remains stationary. You may devise your own topics to be discussed in the pairs such as your favorite rock group, your most embarrassing experience, your favorite place in the world to visit, etc.

7:30 P.M.   Large Group - "Name Game" - Leader:_____.
Have the entire group sit in a large circle. The leader begins by saying his or her name and something he or she likes (for example, 'My name is Bob and I like apples"). The person to the right then repeats what the leader has said and adds something that he or she likes (for example, "His name is Bob and he likes apples; my name is Mary and I like swimming"). The exercise then proceeds around the circle with each previous person and his or her "like" being repeated. This is a fun and challenging way to remember everyone's name from the beginning of the retreat.

8:00 P.M.   Large Group - "Group Division"
The adult in charge should divide the group into small groups of six–eight participants along with two peer ministers to the group. The peer ministers should have decided at their planning sessions with whom they wish to work.

8:10 P.M.   Small Group - "At this moment exercise"
In private rooms, each person in each group is given a pencil and an index card and asked to complete the sentence: "At this moment I am feeling . . ." This exercise allows anxiety or hostility or any lack of ease to surface and perhaps be dispelled in the process.

8:30 P.M.   Talk - "Self-Discovery" - Speaker: _____.
            One of the peer ministers shares with the large group a
            10–15 minute presentation on the process of self-dis-
            covery. It is important that the talk come across not as
            a sermon but rather as a personal disclosure about
            one's own history. All talks delivered on the retreat
            should already have been presented and critiqued dur-
            ing the meeting of the peer ministers.

8:45 P.M.   Small Group - "Symbol Exercise"
            Materials needed: Paper and crayons
            Each person should have a piece of paper and cray-
            ons. Ask the participants to color a symbol of how
            they have changed in the past two years. After all have
            drawn their symbols, share them with the group.

9:30 P.M.   Break

9:45 P.M.   Talk - "Masks" - Speaker:_____.
            It is helpful during talks to light a candle next to the
            speaker and to play an appropriate song related to the
            talk to put people in the correct mood. Soft lighting in
            the conference room can also help to create the
            mood. This talk dwells on the importance of being
            one's self, of not showing a facade of oneself to others,
            and of the need for intimacy if friendships are to devel-
            op. Again personal honesty and the sharing of the
            speaker's own experience are crucial.

10:00 P.M. Small Group - "Discussion"
            Discuss group members' reactions to the talk just giv-
            en. It is usually better if the speaker stays out of the
            small group meeting which immediately follows his or
            her presentation. This allows the group more freedom
            and the speaker some time to rest and regather ener-
            gies.

10:30 P.M. Large Group - "Night Prayer" - Leader:_____ .
The group should sit on the floor in a circle in darkness
with a lighted candle in the center of the group. Open-
ing Song: "Lay Your Burden Down" from the album
Chuck Girard, Myrrh Records, Word Inc., Waco, Tex-
as. Then have an appropriate reading or Scripture passage, with time for private and shared prayer. Closing:
The group joins hands and recites together the Lord's
Prayer. Closing song: "Better Days" by Melissa Man-
chester from her record *Better Days and Happy End-
ings,* Arista Records, Inc.

11:00 P.M. Snack and relaxation

12:00 A.M. Retire

FOLLOWING DAY

8:00 A.M. Rising

9:00 A.M. Breakfast

9:30 A.M. Large Group - "Warm-Up" - Leader: _____ .
If someone plays a guitar, people might sing along or
play "Simon Says" or use "Crowd Breakers" from Lyman Coleman's *Encyclopedia of Serendipity* (Serendipity Press, 1976).

9:45 A.M. Talk - "Our Need for Affirmation" - Speaker:_____ .
In this talk the speaker dwells on the point that we all
need to hear good things about ourselves in order to
like ourselves more and to become more fully who we
are.

10:00 A.M. Large Group - "Affirmation Posters" - Leader:_____ .
Materials needed: Masking tape, poster paper and
dark magic markers.

73

A poster paper is taped on the back of each retreatant. The group is instructed to go to everyone in the room and write one positive comment on the paper without signing it. Appropriate music, such as James Taylor's song "Shower The People," can be played in the background. When everyone is finished, the group should be instructed to sit on the floor and read their posters quietly in the spirit of receiving a gift.

10:45 A.M.   Talk - "The Need for Understanding" - Speaker:_____ .
In this presentation, the speaker discusses the need we all have both to be understood and to understand others in our lives, particularly our parents and friends.

11:00 A.M.   Small Group - "Understanding Exercise"
Materials needed: Index card, pencils
Group members are asked to complete the sentence "I would feel better if I felt that people understood me when I . . ." After each person has completed the index card, he or she shares the statement with the group.

12:00 P.M.   Lunch

12:30 P.M.   Relaxation

1:30 P.M.   Large Group - "Warm-Up"

1:45 P.M.   Talk - "The Friendship of Jesus Christ" - Speaker:_____ .
In this talk, the speaker dwells on the need for a personal relationship with Jesus and again discusses his or her own personal experiences.

2:00 P.M.   Large Group - "Letters from Jesus"
"Letters from Jesus" are passed out. Each retreatant receives a letter with his or her own name. The letter

"LETTER FROM JESUS"

Dear _____

I wanted to send you this letter to tell you how often I think of you and how much I love you. I enjoy it so much when you find time in your busy day to talk with me a little. I'm glad you have your friends and can spend time with them. I guess I'd like to be just as close to you as they are. But I love you even when you never find time to talk with me.

I wonder if you ever realize just how deep my care for you is. It's as deep as the ocean and as wide as the horizon of a desert at sunset. When you feel sometimes drenched by sunlight all over you, think that you are basking in the warmth of my love for you.

When people hurt you and treat you meanly, remember that I know what that feels like. People hurt me a lot, too. And so I'm with you in your problems, whatever they are. I understand.

Lastly, remember that friends, as good as they are, can sometimes be unreliable, just because they're human. But I want you to know you can *always* depend on me. I'll *never* let you down. Ask, seek, knock. I'm here if you want me. You've got a friend.

I love you so much.

Jesus

should be read quietly and the mood can best be preserved by playing a religious song softly in the background.

2:15 P.M. Large Group - "Message-Grams" - Leader:_____ .
Materials needed: Pencil for each participant; four Message-Grams for each participant. The design below should be copied onto $8\frac{1}{2} \times 11$ paper and duplicated.

```
┌─────────────────────────────────────┐
│                                      │
│            Message-Gram              │
│      I want you to know that . . .   │
│                                      │
│                                      │
│      ─────────────────────────       │
│          Signature of sender         │
│                                      │
└─────────────────────────────────────┘
```

The leader explains to the group that sometimes it's easier to compliment each other in this exercise than it is verbally. Each group member should receive one message-gram which has on it the name of some *other* member of the large group. He or she is instructed to write something positive to that person in the space provided and to sign the message-gram. This assignment of the initial message-gram is essential to ensure that everyone on the retreat receives one message. Each retreatant is then given three more message-grams that he or she may send to anyone else in the large group. Everyone should then go quietly to his or her room or some quiet place to write the personal message. Stress that these messages are to be positive and affirming.

2:45 P.M. Small Group - "Good Qualities Exercise"
The entire small group focuses on one person at a time, and each other member of the group mentions

76

some good quality observed about that person particularly in the course of these twenty-four hours.

3:45 P.M.   Break

4:00 P.M.   Large Group - "Open Message-Grams"
Closing remarks - Leader:_____ .
Whatever the chief leader of the weekend feels appropriate to sum up this twenty-four hours may be commented on at this time. As quiet music is played, the peer ministers then distribute all the message-grams to each member of the large group. At this point the group should be seated on the floor with a lighted candle in the middle. People can be invited to respond to senders by getting up and going over to thank them or kiss them or shake hands or whatever seems appropriate. (There should be no pressure to do this.)

4:30 P.M.   Large Group - "Closing Prayer Service or Liturgy"
Leader:_____ .
If there is no liturgy, a prayer service similar to the night prayer of the previous evening may be used. A song is a good way to end, sung by the group standing arm in arm.

5:00 P.M.   Clean-up

5:30 P.M.   Supper

7:00 P.M.   Departure

GROUND-RULES FOR PERSONAL GROWTH RETREAT
(and other group experiences for peer ministers when on team)

1. Exercise leadership and responsibility by your courteous response to the adult leaders' directives. Be prompt when requested, generous in helping with preparations and clean-up, and cooperative when it is time to retire for the night.
2. Do not bring any alcohol or drugs or other distractions and be alert to this possibility among the participants.
3. Talk to new people outside your own group; try to help others feel comfortable. Most importantly, if you have a boyfriend or girlfriend in the peer ministry group, make the deliberate sacrifice to keep your distance until the closing.
4. Be friendly and polite. *Your behavior will be observed* (whether you realize it or not) and will set the tone for others.

POINTERS FOR TALKS ON "PERSONAL GROWTH RETREAT"

1. "Self-Discovery"
(a) Talk about yourself as a younger child; give examples.
(b) Trace your development over the past two years; give examples.
(c) Share a hope for yourself in the future.

(This talk sets the tone for the level of honest communication on the retreat. It should be very open and honest.)

2. "Masks"
(a) Give examples of how people are phony.

(b) Share some personal examples of "masks" or facades which you wear.

(c) Discuss the retreat *and* the Christian community as places where it's "O.K." to be your real self—places of acceptance and love.

3. "Our Need for Affirmation"
(a) Mention affirming signs that make us feel good.

(b) Discuss your own personal need for affirmation by way of examples.

(c) Stress the value of physical touch in making us feel affirmed.

4. "The Need for Understanding"
(a) Discuss your own experience of *not* being understood by family members and friends. Give personal examples.

(b) Explain ways of making another feel understood by you (e.g., listening).

(c) Relate being understood to the freeing feeling of being open and courageous in the face of the future, e.g., we are given the security we need to continue to grow.

5. "The Friendship of Jesus Christ"
(a) Discuss qualities of human friendship in your life; be personal.

(b) Relate these qualities to your love for Jesus and his love for you.

(c) Challenge and invite each person in the group to try to feel Jesus' love more fully by spending some time with him in prayer. (Bear in mind that many kids on the retreat may never have had an experience of God's love on the feeling level. Tell them what is offered to them.)

4 | PRACTICAL CONSIDERATIONS FOR PEER MINISTRY

SETTING UP A PEER MINISTRY PROGRAM: A PARISH APPROACH

It is often easiest to begin a peer ministry program around a confirmation program in a parish. Presuming that the sacrament is administered in the ninth or tenth grade, peer ministers can be initially enlisted among upperclassmen for the formation of the confirmation candidates. This rationale for enlisting help inspires a healthy sense of self-importance in the older teenagers. Adults need to admit that they can't do a successful program alone, but that they honestly need the peer ministers to "get through" to kids in ways that they themselves cannot. The best approach at first is simply to request an older group of teenagers to help you in this venture. They should be approached individually and *personally*.

This method is far superior to putting an announcement in the parish bulletin. The young people asked should be active members of the parish who have a life of faith to some degree. It is additionally helpful if some of them are natural leaders in the school community (e.g., a football star or a class officer). This dimension will enhance the credibility of the entire enterprise with the younger people.

Thus we have said that in the initial stages it is best:

1. to enlist peer ministers to work in a concrete program;
2. to invite them personally to join;
3. *initially,* to include *some* teenagers who enjoy a wide respect.

The first order of business is to begin to build a community among the peer ministers through the Initial Leaders' Workshop or a similar retreat experience. It is then important that they begin to work immediately with the underclassmen to help them establish a sense of identity. Therefore a commissioning ceremony would be appropriate right away. As to their work itself, it would begin by having planning sessions with involved adults regarding programs, retreats, etc., in which the peer ministers could help by giving talks, running groups, organizing liturgies, etc. The time lapse between the Initial Leaders' Workshop and the first program in which the peer ministers assist shouldn't be more than about a month.

Then *after* some service has occurred, both the personal growth meetings and the training sessions will assume more significance. The personal growth meeting is the most important time the peer ministers spend together because it is in being a group *member* that one learns to be a group *leader* by growing in awareness and understanding of human interaction.

Note that we are indicating that the training sessions be interspersed throughout an academic year along with planning and personal sessions. We suggest this only for the first year of a peer ministry program in a parish. Our premise is that the identity of peer ministry is being established. Once it *is* established and moves out of its infancy, the training sessions can be required of peer ministry candidates the semester or summer before their actual commissioning. However we still suggest the ebb and flow of planning—personal—educational sessions throughout any year of peer ministry. The difference is that educational sessions can be more sophisticated than the training sessions and can help the ministers learn to function more effectively in group work, public speaking, and counseling skills. It should also be noted that occasional sessions devoted in large part to prayer are important for the spiritual development of the group.

After peer ministry has been established/accepted in a parish, there need not be an arduous effort to solicit kids to join. Underclassmen, in the confirmation model suggested earlier, will begin to view peer ministry as something to aspire to, as a position of Christian maturity after reception of the sacrament. If the original group of peer ministers has worked effectively there should be an ample number of aspirants among the underclassmen.

FIVE YEARS: LOOKING BACK

The following are five very practical hints for success for the parish peer ministry program based on five years of experience in the same parish.

1. Limit the group to 10–12 members.
2. Be selective. The reception of the sacrament of con-

firmation does not fulfill requirements for membership. The application form and a personal interview are essential.

3. There are problems if members of a previous peer ministry group are joined by newer members. The group has a new composition and can never duplicate the original group for the older members. While comparison to former groups can at times be problematic, the benefit of continuity generally outweighs this difficulty.

4. If a clique develops within the group, it should be faced openly within a group personal growth session.

5. Stick to the same evening of the week for peer ministry meetings, as young people find it easier to develop patterns at the outset of the school year.

A HIGH SCHOOL APPROACH

Many of the same approaches can be used within the Catholic high school as within the parish. A simple model might be seniors working with freshman religion classes and retreats.

The following are ten very practical hints for a successful peer ministry program; they come from a teacher who has worked with peer ministry in a school for ten years:

1. Go around and make a brief presentation to upperclassmen and upperclasswomen on the program and be sure they know that it is open to all. The presentation should give them a general idea of what it is all about and general responsibilities.

2. Call a meeting of any interested people at a free period during the day. At this meeting, give them a handout explaining the program, and give more details about it.

3. Post a schedule near your office, and tell them at this meeting that if they are still interested, they are to meet with you in a one-to-one interview. They can sign up on the schedule at your office. The interview can involve what you wish, but be sure to meet with them and allow for no excuses. After these initial meetings, you will eliminate a lot of individuals who otherwise might be interested but who are not responsible enough to be there when needed. In addition to the interview, use the application form for peer ministry found in the appendix of this book.

4. Hand out evaluation sheets on those who have made it through the interview to teachers, administrators, and guidance counselors. These evaluations should be considered confidential and only consultative in nature. Be sure you let the evaluator know both of these factors when you give him or her a form. Again, it is good to know teachers, administrators, and counselors so that you can easily talk to them about individual candidates and be able to separate personal baggage that they may have from information that might be useful to you.

5. At this point decide who your peer ministers are going to be. Try not to have a group any larger than twelve. Do not be afraid to say "no" to individuals, or you'll pay the price later. You should have told them in the beginning that the group will have to be small, but you should try to be as honest as possible with individuals as to why you have said "no" to them.

6. The first meeting with the group should occur within the week: don't wait too long or they'll sense that you don't mean business. At this meeting, give them a detailed handout on the program and their responsibility in it. Announce to them the dates of the peer ministry initial workshop as well as their explicit responsibilities throughout the semester.

7. The subsequent meetings should involve workshops, training, etc., with outside help. *You can't do it alone.* You are not to build up your own kingdom, or you'll alienate a lot

85

of people who will not be there afterward when you need their help. It is very important that you get the help of the guidance department. In all of the initial training, be sure that the ministers realize that they are not guidance counselors themselves.

8. Peer ministers should work with underclassmen and underclasswomen. They could be attached to religion classes or helpful in campus ministry programs such as retreats and experiential workshops. If they work in the classroom, they can best run small groups and give talks from the front of the room as individuals or as teams. Some of the topics that can be approached are life adjustment, growth, values, relationship and faith sharing. They have a lot of personal experience to share. Peers should be left alone at times. Let's face it: some issues just won't surface with the teacher there all the time. You have to trust them, *but* be sure to have them give you feed-back on what's happening in the class.

9. Be careful that these peers are sensitive to the fact that underclassmen and underclasswomen are not where they are at! Patience is a great virtue here. Sometimes peers become more impatient than adults with younger people. Be sure that the peers always explain fully what they are talking about when talking to groups. Ideally, it would be good to have a room set aside where underclassmen and underclasswomen could do some "hanging out" with these peers. A lot can happen outside the classroom. Again, be sure that peers know that they are not guidance counselors, and if things seem to be going in that direction, they have to be willing to refer a student to someone who is trained to help or they could do real harm.

10. You should meet every week with peer ministers for at least an hour to keep them up to date on where you are going in the classroom. It is advisable to meet outside of the school day!

These weekly meetings should be mini-training sessions, but time should also be given for a discussion of where the peer counselors are at. You should do a lot with peer ministers—go away for a weekend retreat, etc. *Whatever you do,* try not to meet with them during the day in school schedule. Meet at another time. This is important! Being a peer minister is not just taking another course for an easy grade. Books should be assigned and articles handed out for them to read. Let them know that this is serious business. Give them feedback on how they are doing. At the end of a quarter, have them evaluate themselves in writing. Have their "students" evaluate them in writing and give these to them. Meet with them on an individual basis and talk about things. *Give them your evaluations.* You should meet with them individually throughout the year. It would be ideal to share time with them in other school activities to help you know them better, and to help you know you better. *You can be a real team* if you share a lot together. You *cannot* be just the organizer of a program; you have to be involved with the peers. You cannot work with individuals you don't know.

THE T-SHIRT

One way to help the peer ministry group to become cohesive is to provide each member with a T-shirt with a common insignia or emblem. Light blue seems to be a favorite color for the T-shirt of both boys and girls alike. The shirt also provides the group with corporate visibility which in turn enhances their role of leadership.

A FOOTNOTE ON SOCIAL JUSTICE

While it is not the purpose of this book to provide programming for parish and schools, we wish to give a word of advice. Most youth programs in North America take into account emotional growth, spiritual development, and socializing or fellowship. One of the weaknesses of many programs is that youth are not deeply concerned with grave social issues facing our world beyond the level of tokenism. Peer ministers can provide a great service by encouraging social awareness in others after they themselves have been sensitized. The following, excerpted from "Orientciones para la Pastoral Juvenil en Chile" by the National Commission for Youth Ministry in Santiago, Chile, in 1977, is worthy of reflection. We have much to learn from our brothers and sisters in Latin America.

- To value everything that is positive and good that is done for the good of man and of mankind coming from whomever;
- to contribute with total initiative to that which is recorded in the kingdom of God and to oppose prophetically all that is an obstacle;
- to know how to penetrate the causes of the problems that the youth tries to solve—all this means, in reality, a fight for the integral liberation of all enslaved youth and of all sin.
- In a word, the Christian youth assume the mission given by the Lord to be the yeast of this world encouraging or promoting every action or search for peace, of equality of justice and of brotherhood, without yielding to the anti-evangelical. . . .

REMARKS BY PEER MINISTERS

Being a part of this group has given me a way to share myself openly with others, and to discover that sharing my experiences helps me and other kids to grow in self-acceptance. I've always wanted to grow closer to others, and I've found that working with them in a situation like this brings us closer together in a real way. (*Bill*)

The leadership group has been a real growing experience for me. It has been a chance to share deeply and confidentially with other people, and it has also given me the chance to help others engage in retreat and sharing experiences. I think the major asset to membership in such a group is: one has the chance, as a member, to explore deeper one's real self as well as another's without fear of being laughed at or rejected. It has been a truly beneficial support group for me. (*Andy*)

Sharing is a very special quality, and can be brought to a deeper realm with practice. Being a leader in the Leadership Group has brought me to this deeper realm. Being a leader in any way requires responsibility, awareness and an open mind. One no longer thinks only of one's own feelings, but those of others become more and more clear. Sometimes it's scary to know you must be on your toes because others are watching or listening, but this is a challenge. Being a leader is becoming a better person in all ways! I enjoy it very much. (*Kathy*)

APPENDIX

RESOURCES FOR YOUTH MINISTERS

Peer Training:

Peer Program for Youth by Ardyth Hebeisen, Augsburg Publishing House, 1973.

Extend: Youth Reaching Youth by Kenneth Fletcher, *et al.,* Augsburg, 1974.

Becoming the Gift by Dorothy Williams. This is a project of the National Forum for Religious Educators at NCEA in cooperation with the Youth Research Center of Minneapolis, Minnesota, 1975.

The Complete Handbook of Peer Counseling by Don and Mimi Samuels, Fiesta Publishing Corporation, 1975.

"We Did It Ourselves," *Youth Magazine,* Vol. 27, Nos. 7 and 8, July—August, 1976.

"Peer Group Counseling: A Total School Approach," by Wayne Dyer, *et al., Momentum,* December 1975, pp. 8–15.

Text:

Good News From Matthew by Joseph Moore, Liguori Publications, 1978. An easy-to-use weekly program with twenty-three lessons from the New Testament designed for older teenagers.

Other:

Resources for Youth Ministry by Michael Warren, ed., Paulist Press, 1978.

Young Adult Ministry Resources, Department of Education, United States Catholic Conference, 1977.

Portrait of Youth Ministry by Maria Harris, Paulist Press, 1981.

Periodicals:

The following periodicals contain excellent ideas for training peer ministers or provide helpful material.

Essence of Adolescence
168 Woodbridge Avenue
Highland Park, N.J. 08904
$9.00

Group
P.O. Box 481
Loveland, Col. 80537
$12.50

Youthletter
1716 Spruce Street
Philadelphia, Pa. 19103
$8.50 yearly

Resources for Youth Ministry
500 N. Broadway
St. Louis, Mo. 63102
$7.00 per year

RESOURCES FOR PEER MINISTERS

The following books have excellent suggestions for activities
and exercises which can be used for the peer minister group
itself or by the peer minister in planning activities for others.

Encyclopedia of Serendipity by Lyman Coleman, Serendipity
   House, 1976.
Awareness Experiences for School Use by Bette Hamlin,
   Pflaum Publishing, 1975.
Awareness: Exploring, Experimenting, Experiencing by John
   O. Stevens, Real People Press, 1971.
Designs in Affective Education by Elizabeth W. Flynn and
   John F. LaFaso, Paulist Press, 1974.
Get Away From It All—Have a Retreat, Young Calvinist Fed-
   eration, 1976.
*The Good Times Game Book—Good Things For Youth
   Leaders,* Young Calvinist Federation, 1977.
Taking Charge of Your Life by Leland W. How, Argus Com-
   munications, 1977.
Meeting Yourself Halfway by Dr. Sidney B. Simon, Argus
   Communications, 1974.
Search for Meaning. Center for Learning, Inc.
Sharing 9, 10, 11/12 by Thomas Zanzig, St. Mary's Press,
   1979.
The Best of Try This One by Thom Schultz, Group Magazine,
   1977.

SELECTION PROCESS

It is important to realize that everyone who applies to be a peer minister should not be accepted solely on the grounds of that desire. Careful consideration should be given to the ability a person *already* has to relate to his or her peers and to the recommendations by significant adults who know the applicant. Proceeding on the basis of recommendations helps to preserve objectivity. It is true that refusal of an applicant can result in hurt feelings, but this is far less problematic than future situations may be if the candidate is accepted. We can confirm this by our experience. A final suggestion to adult leaders: Encourage your people who are *already* leaders among their peer group (e.g., a football or cheerleading captain) to apply. Peer ministry as an institution becomes more acceptable when endorsed and participated in by respected members of the youth community.

Dear Prospective Peer Minister,

Welcome to the beginning of a very important phase of your spiritual, human life. The course of peer ministry upon which you are about to embark holds great promise for you. You are standing on a frontier of unleashed potential. The Spirit of Jesus within you awaits being expanded. There are many young people in your community of friends-to-be awaiting your influence. Please take seriously the commitment and challenge before you.

You may begin your new ministry by completing the application form. (Do not use your parents as the recommending adults.)

Exercise responsibility by returning this form by the assigned date.

Peace and the love of Christ

PEER MINISTRY APPLICATION FORM

Name _____Age_____Grade _____
School _____Parish _____

Please respond *realistically* and *honestly:*

1. What strengths do you see in yourself that would contribute to your effectiveness as a peer minister?_____
   _____
   _____
   _____.

2. Are you willing to give priority to our weekly meeting on _____ night over work or other commitments?

3. Can you attend all the retreats, workshops and personal growth days in the calendar for this school year?

4. Write a brief paragraph about your philosophy of peer ministry. _____
   _____
   _____
   _____.

5. Who are two adults who you feel are in a position to recommend you for this work?
   Name _____Phone _____
   Name _____Phone _____

COMMISSIONING CEREMONY

This ceremony should be witnessed by members of the parish or school community, and is preferably celebrated within a liturgy. By so doing, the commitment to peer ministry remains no longer simply an individual decision; it becomes a public act. This is very important as a reinforcement in an age where commitment is increasingly difficult. Also, it strengthens the faith of the adult members of the community to witness the dedication of the young. An appropriate point in the eucharistic liturgy would be right after the homily. The peer ministry candidates could come forth into the sanctuary as their names are called by a lector. If each individual is given a lighted candle, the ceremony is enhanced. If a cross necklace is to be distributed, the candidates should kneel. After the commissioning itself, the kiss of peace from the pastor and/or youth minister and applause from the congregation symbolizes the acceptance by the community of this important ministry within the Church.

The following is a sample of a brief commissioning ceremony:

LEADER: (Peer ministers are kneeling holding lit candles)

Christian leadership is a desirable commodity in our age where material things have very often become more important than people, and where commitment is often replaced by convenience.

The ___(church name)___ parish community is very encouraged by our youth leadership group and the young adults who work with them. Thus it is with pride and joy and hope that we commission you people tonight to continue to minister to your peers throughout your lifetimes.

(the leader places a cross around the neck of each peer minister and says:)

___(Name)___, wear this cross as a symbol of your own unselfishness and your feeling for Jesus, bread for your journey.

EVALUATIONS

Evaluations are a key to growth in any endeavor. Often others can see our strengths and weaknesses better than we can ourselves. Ongoing evaluations of the peer minister by adults with whom he or she works and young people to whom he or she has ministered can be of great benefit. Honesty, even when it hurts, should be received as a gift from a person who cares enough to be interested in our growth.

It is recommended that the peer minister be evaluated once per semester by two adults with whom he or she works and by two young people, randomly chosen, to whom he or she has ministered. Written evaluations, after they have been read, *should always be discussed with the evaluator* for further clarification and to prevent misunderstanding.

YOUTH EVALUATION OF PEER MINISTER

1. Ways in which the peer minister affected me or had a positive influence on me: _____
_____
_____
_____

2. A way in which I feel the peer minister could improve his or her ministry: _____
_____
_____
_____.

3. Concluding remarks: _____
_____
_____
_____.

Name _____ Date _____

Occasion on which I observed the peer minister in a leadership capacity: _____
_____
_____
_____.

ADULT EVALUATION OF PEER MINISTER

1. Strengths I have observed in him or her. _____
   _____
   _____
   _____ .

2. Areas in his or her ministry in which I see room for growth. Please elaborate. _____
   _____
   _____
   _____ .

3. Concluding remarks: _____
   _____
   _____
   _____ .

School/Parish _____
Name _____Date _____

I have known the peer minister for _____ ,
(time) and worked with him or her for _____ .

PEER MINISTER'S PERFORMANCE LOG

A helpful *self-evaluation* tool can be the faithful keeping of a personal log. Keep track of all the events in which you exercised your ministry of leadership.

Event: _____.

Place: _____.

Date: _____.

Something I learned about myself: _____.

An area in which I can improve: _____.

An improvement I noticed since my last experience: _____.

*   *   *

Event: _____.

Place: _____.

Date: _____.

Something I learned about myself: _____.

An area in which I can improve: _____.

An improvement I noticed since my last experience: _____.

Event: _____.